The ALMOST No Cholesterol GOURMET Cookbook

Also by

Jeannette M. Seaver

**Jeannette's Secrets
of Everyday Good Cooking**

Soups

The ALMOST No Cholesterol Gourmet Cookbook

Foreword by Jeremiah A. Barondess, M.D.
William T. Foley Distinguished Professor of Clinical Medicine,
Cornell University Medical College,
and President, New York Academy of Medicine

Under the medical supervision of Harold L. Karpman, M.D., F.A.C.P., F.A.C.C.
Associate Clinical Professor of Medicine, U.C.L.A. School of Medicine,
and Elizabeth A. Baron, R.D.

Jeannette M. Seaver

Illustrations by Nathalie Seaver

Crown Publishers, Inc., New York

Designed by Nancy Kenmore
Illustrations by Nathalie Seaver
Copyright © 1990 by Jeannette M. Seaver
Foreword copyright © 1990 by
Jeremiah A. Barondess, M.D.

Published by Crown Publishers, Inc.,
201 East 50th Street, New York, New York 10022.
Member of the Crown Publishing Group.

CROWN is a trademark of Crown Publishers, Inc.

Manufactured in the United States of America

Library of Congress Cataloging-in-Publication Data
Seaver, Jeannette.
The (almost) no cholesterol gourmet cookbook/by
Jeannette M. Seaver; foreword by Jeremiah A.
Barondess.—1st ed.
p.   cm.
"With the medical supervision of Harold L.
Karpman, M.D., Director, Cardiovascular Medical
Group of Southern California."
1. Low-cholesterol diet—Recipes.   I. Title.
RM237.75.S43   1990
641.5'6311—dc20   89-25268
CIP
ISBN 0-517-57518-3
10   9   8   7   6   5   4   3   2   1
First Edition

To Dick,

who inspired this book

and who, despite the cholesterol alert,

consistently inspired

our daily gastronomy.

Contents

Foreword

*I*n recent years, Americans have turned their attention more and more to matters of health, and in this widening concern diet now occupies the most prominent place. We've come a long way from the days when the physical dimensions achieved by, say, President William Howard Taft were regarded as a benign normal variant; or when elaborate dinners of six, eight, or even more heavy courses were viewed as proper expressions of a cook's talents or reassurances of the abundance of nature and the wealth of the nation. What has emerged is a broadening consensus among the public and those in medicine that the size and composition of one's diet are major contributors to one's health, and that they are intimately linked to one's prospects for a longer and more healthy life.

Among the potential impacts of diet attracting most attention, the effect on blood levels of cholesterol is most significant. The cholesterol content of the blood bears heavily on the health of one's arteries, and this in turn influences one's risk of acquiring or dying from a number of distressingly common diseases, especially atheromatosis (arteriosclerosis) of the coronary, cerebral, and peripheral arteries.

How big is that risk? In this country about 1.5 million heart attacks occur annually—that is, about 4,000 per day, or 3 per minute—resulting in more than 500,000 deaths. In addition, about a half-million strokes afflict Americans each year and result in more than 175,000 deaths.

That modification of personal habits can have a positive effect on health is suggested by the fact that in the last twenty to thirty years the frequency of coronary heart disease has been falling, and most physicians believe this is due to increasing national attention to health and hygiene, as expressed in personal exercise programs, modifications of diet, and cessation of cigarette smoking. Nevertheless, the diseases resulting from arteriosclerosis are still disturbingly common. Heart disease remains the third most common cause of death in the United States, and most of these deaths are due to arteriosclerosis of the coronary arteries.

A number of factors predispose people to both heart attack and stroke: elevated blood cholesterol levels, high blood pressure, and cigarette smoking prominently; obesity, diabetes, and a sedentary life-style secondarily, but also important. Of these factors, cholesterol levels have been the primary focus of efforts to improve health through diet, and properly so. While avoidance of obesity is also important in controlling health risks, and restriction of salt intake is helpful in managing some instances of high blood pressure, reduction of serum cholesterol concentration is likely to be the most effective risk-reduction intervention an individual can make. This change cannot be accomplished without modifying the traditional American diet.

The new dietary efforts are based on many observations, in both humans and experimental animals, that link high blood cholesterol levels with development and progression of the arterial lesions (atheromas) of arteriosclerosis. These cholesterol-containing plaques tend to appear relatively early in life; they can, in fact, be found in their early stages in the arteries of many American teenagers, for example. Atheromas tend to progress slowly, increasing in size and extent over the ensuing decades. Ultimately, if they become severe, the arterial canal may be narrowed, sometimes to such a degree that, with or without the deposition of a superimposed blood clot, the artery is completely blocked. When this occurs, the tissue fed by the occluded artery loses its blood supply and is damaged. The clinical result depends on the size and location of the involved artery. If it is a branch of a coronary artery, for example, the patch of heart muscle it supplies is affected; if it is a cerebral artery, the area of the brain it normally nourishes is damaged. Under other circumstances, particularly in individuals with high blood pressure, atheromatous arteries, especially in the brain, may leak or rupture, resulting in one variety of stroke.

It is important to understand that cholesterol is a normal and essential body constituent, required for the synthesis of vitamin D, a number of hormones, and cell walls; and for the manufacture of bile acids, which are important components of the digestive process. For most of us, the amount of cholesterol in the blood far exceeds the needs of the body, and can be sharply reduced without compromising any vital process. In the healthy person, the blood level of cholesterol is determined largely by the rate at which it is made by the liver. For the most part, this rate is under genetic control, usually about 1,500 to 2,000 milligrams (½₀ of an ounce) of cholesterol a day. The contribution to cholesterol levels made by diet is superimposed on this, and adds about a third more to the quantity made by the liver. It is this extra quantity that can be somewhat regulated through dietary means.

Cholesterol doesn't circulate free in the blood, but is carried on a number of proteins. The major carrier is low-density lipoprotein, known familiarly as LDL. The level of LDL is directly related to cardiovascular risk. the other major carrier, high-density lipoprotein (HDL), transports about 25 percent of blood cholesterol; its level is inversely related to cardiovascular risk, although the mechanism of its protective effect is still unclear. Currently both LDL and HDL levels are measured along with total serum cholesterol; the additional information gained is useful in evaluating risk and following responses to diet or other interventions.

Diet has a major effect on LDL levels, which rise in response to high intakes of cholesterol and saturated fats and fall when these are reduced. HDL levels appear to be under tighter genetic control and are generally more stable, although exercise and moderate alcohol intake tend to raise them. Men tend to have higher LDL and lower HDL levels than women, probably owing to sex hormone effects. In general, blood cholesterol levels rise with age.

Foods high in cholesterol and saturated fats have long occupied a prominent place in the American diet, which contains, on average, a daily dose of about 800 milligrams of cholesterol and derives about 40 to 45 percent of its calories from fats. Studies in the last few years have resulted in the recommendation that dietary intake of cholesterol should be markedly reduced, that fats should contribute about 30 percent of total calories, and that these should be made up largely of polyunsaturated fats.

Foods containing large amounts of cholesterol and saturated fats include egg yolks, shellfish, red meats, and rich dairy products. Polyunsaturated fats include corn oil, soybean oil, and some fish oils.

It is abundantly clear that the dietary changes described here can reduce levels of total and LDL cholesterol in the circulating blood, sometimes substantially, and can hold them there. Many individuals have been able to reduce elevated levels to normal through dietary means alone. Others have added quantities of oat bran or fish oils to their daily intakes, and yet others have used prescription medications when dietary efforts produce insufficient results. The crucial point is that none of these additional maneuvers, medications included, is effective without the basic changes in eating patterns that reduce an individual's intake of cholesterol and saturated fats and increase the proportion of daily calories derived from unsaturated fats.

As millions know, changing one's lifetime eating patterns isn't easy. Nevertheless, many people are doing so: recent studies have shown a 36 percent decrease in the consumption of butter in this country in the last two decades, along with a 15 percent fall in the intake of eggs and an increase of 74 percent in the consumption of vegetable fats and oils.

For most people the ultimate issue is how to do it—how to eat prudently and protect one's arteries, but still eat pleasurably and well. Given the facts, it remains for intelligent and talented cooks like Jeannette Seaver to show the way. Having had the good fortune to sit at her table and sample many of the recipes in this volume, I am delighted to report that it really is possible to eat superbly and protect your health simultaneously. *Bon appétit!*

Jeremiah A. Barondess, M.D.

William T. Foley Distinguished Professor
of Clinical Medicine,
Cornell University Medical College, and
President, New York Academy of Medicine

Introduction

$\mathcal{F}$ ine cooking is an art . . ." I wrote some fifteen years ago in the opening sentence of my first cookbook. I still stand firmly behind that statement. Cooking indeed remains an art—one practiced, I might add, by many millions more than it was a decade and a half ago—but an art that has evolved. The intrusion of cholesterol has altered radically—and irreversibly—the very foundation of gastronomy, at least for me. The art of classic French cooking is predicated on rich ingredients such as cream, butter, eggs (and more eggs!), pork fat, liver, and marrow, to name but a few of the culprits. Just take two of the basic elements of French cuisine—*crème patissière* (pastry cream) and hollandaise sauce. *Crème patissière* is the basis for half the wonderful cakes and pastries of France. What does it consist of? Egg yolks (many!) and whole milk, not to mention butter. Hollandaise sauce? It's basically egg yolks, and again butter. Another of the unique charms of French cuisine, of course, is the infinite variety of rich pâtés. And what goes into making a good pâté? Innards, cream, butter, eggs, and pork fat. Any one of these ingredients figures on the anti-cholesterol "Ten Most Wanted List."

Over the past twenty years or so we have seen French cuisine conquer the United States. Witness the thousands upon thousands of gourmet restaurants, the hundreds of cooking schools, the countless cookbooks, and now the many television programs. More recently, however, an unwelcome new element has appeared on the scene to dampen the culinary euphoria: cholesterol. It now seems convincingly clear from all the evidence that the "cholesterol problem" is more than a passing scare. It is an undisputed fact. High cholesterol is a major—if not preeminent—cause of heart attack in the Western world.

It is also clear that modification of diet often can positively affect the cho-lesterol level of people in high-risk categories. Unfortunately, the people in this category number in the millions. As Robert Kowalski notes in his best-selling book *The 8-Week Cholesterol Cure*, "Certainly diet is the first step toward controlling levels of total cholesterol in the blood."

After a long, thoroughly enjoyable life of daily gastronomic celebration to-gether, my husband and I joined the high-risk cholesterol group. "You've abso-lutely got to change your eating habits," our doctor told us, "and at once. I could put you on medication, but I prefer not to, at least for now." Instead, we were given a three-month probation period.

If we were upset by the news of our unacceptably high cholesterol levels, we were even more distressed at the thought of reducing our evening feasts to bland (or even distasteful) anti-cholesterol essentials. For me, cooking had always been fun—both an art and a celebration, a necessary part of my life. But if we were now doomed to a spartan diet of celery and carrots, bran muffins, and Lord knows what else, life would lose much of its charm. I immediately began to have sinful gastronomic visions: a panoply of rich pâtés; buttery tarts, made with my butter-cream pie crust; blinis with caviar, sour cream, *and* melted butter; egg-laden brioches stuffed with warm marrow.

Having grown up in France and having learned my basic cooking skills there, I confess that my first book—the thrust of which was to make classic French cuisine accessible by simplifying the recipes and cutting down on the time spent in the kitchen—did nothing to solve America's cholesterol problem. The thought of giving up that cuisine was almost more than I could bear. On the other hand, I would be a fool to ignore my doctor's dire warning. So for the next two or three weeks we went on an anti-cholesterol crash diet: no eggs, no cheese, no pork, no red meat, no butter, no whole milk. In their stead came a succession of dishes that no amount of disguising could render appetizing or palatable. Thus while our dangerous cholesterol level was declining slowly, our morale was sinking rapidly. Cooking, which till now had been a daily pleasure, overnight became an ordeal. I had reached the point where I virtually was ready to call the doctor and capitulate:

he could put us on medication if, in turn, we could go on a less stringent and onerous diet.

It was then that I decided that "eating to survive" was just not in my nature. The French often are accused of "living to eat"—an accusation not far from the truth. How to adapt the present situation to that dictum—how to cook delicious gourmet meals *and* lower our cholesterol—was the challenge. Without wasting another day, I set out to invent, adapt, and test recipes that would qualify as gourmet and still reduce our cholesterol levels. For several months I experimented obsessively, but with increasing success. Some substitutes did not work, but others did wonderfully. The more than 200 recipes that follow are the product of that research and testing.

I suspect my breakthrough came the day I made a bouillabaisse with three different kinds of mayonnaise—regular, an ailloli (aioli), and a rouille—without using a single egg yolk, and it was as good a bouillabaisse as I'd ever made. Encouraged, I pursued my no-egg, no-butter cuisine with a vengeance: various pâtés with elegant sauces, absolutely cholesterol free; a wide range of tarts made with a mouth-watering pie crust that was both yolkless and butterless; even cream puffs without cream. I went on to make everything from sausages to soufflés, all cholesterol safe.

The first real test of my new "gourmet diet" was a dinner party for eight, at which I served nothing but cholesterol-free dishes. I served course after course, and each elicited the same hearty response that I looked for in my classic-cooking days. Only at the very end of the meal did I reveal to my guests that they had probably eaten one of the most healthful meals of their lives.

Although this book emanates from an urgent personal situation, current estimates are that a third—and perhaps as much as a half—of the Western world suffers from high cholesterol. Thus while I write essentially for this rather significant segment of the population, this book also serves those who are not at risk but who would like to ensure that their cholesterol levels stay acceptable. The recipes here are as elegant, imaginative, and I believe delicious as those in any standard cookbook; the difference is that they are cholesterol-proof, or virtually so.

One caution: this book is not a low-sodium, low-fat diet book. However, anyone who desires to can easily adapt the recipes by reducing or eliminating both fats and salts. The reader will also note that throughout this book I have made liberal use of garlic. I have done so for two reasons: First, I like it and I have found that, when used judiciously in appropriate dishes, garlic imparts an irresistible and rich aroma that transforms the dullest recipe into a feast. Second, although medical experts differ as to the medicinal and therapeutic effects of the garlic, increasing evidence suggests a solid base for the folklore. Those who do not share my gastronomic enthusiasm for garlic can rest assured that most of the recipes can be successfully prepared without it.

As my husband and I learned, keeping your cholesterol at a level consistent with good health not only is desirable but is essential, whatever your age. Even young people are susceptible to the problem, we are learning. It is also a fact that far too few people know their cholesterol count, and should have their level checked as soon as possible. Fortunately, if you have a cholesterol problem you *can* do something about it. Most people can dramatically reduce cholesterol levels through diet. This book aims to accomplish that goal of diet modification without sacrificing pleasure at mealtime.

In keeping with the principles of my earlier books, the recipes here can, almost without exception, be prepared with a minimum of time and effort. This is a book of haute cuisine, but I urge the reader not to be deterred by any recipes that seem at first glance daunting or complicated. They are not. In each instance I have sought to find ways of rendering each recipe as delicious as its cholesterol-laden counterpart.

Because I received so much mail from users of my earlier cookbooks, who thanked me for combining recipes into full menus, I have focused this book on full menus, some thirty dinner menus and ten lunch menus in all. Some are two-course, some three-course, some four. They are recipes I think work especially well together, always keeping in mind balance of texture, appearance, substance, and aroma. Obviously, however, you can substitute one or more courses in any given menu, depending on your tastes and desires of the day, and on the availability of produce. The trick in this project was to find safe substitutes for all the major cholesterol culprits, without sacrificing taste or texture. For instance, wherever eggs are called for in the classic cuisine I use egg whites from medium to large eggs mixed with evaporated skim milk, or commercial egg substitutes. The results are amazingly good, whether in morning pancakes, French crepes, cakes, sauces, quiches, or—believe it or not—omelettes!

Having had to eliminate all manner of creams—crème fraîche, sour cream, heavy cream, and half-and-half—not to mention butter, I replace them with a variety of creative substitutes. For sour cream, for example, I combine 1% cottage cheese with low-fat yogurt. Heavy cream—since it is used so often—posed an especially thorny problem. After a number of experiments, however, I came up with the following solution: soy milk (which has absolutely no cholesterol) used in varying thicknesses as required. For butter, I naturally use polyunsaturated margarine and, as often as possible, olive oil.

For my pie crust, I have often opted for filo dough, which is available in most stores and markets, since it is fat free. Alternatively, I make puff pastry with polyunsaturated margarine. As for regular pie crust, I use low-fat cream cheese or 1% cottage cheese combined with polyunsaturated margarine.

I have long made my own sausages, but whereas once I used pork and pork fat, now I make sausages just as tasty using ground turkey or chicken breast—and I defy anyone to tell the difference!

There are many varieties of vinaigrettes; here, I have stayed close to the classic ones. Some people prefer peanut oil to olive oil and, again, some people like a touch of sugar in their dressing while others enjoy garlic. Here are the vinaigrettes referred to in this book:

Vinaigrette with Wine Vinegar

•

1 tablespoon wine vinegar
2 teaspoons Dijon-style mustard
3 tablespoons olive oil
   Fresh black pepper and salt to taste

Balsamic Vinaigrette

•

1 tablespoon Balsamic vinegar
2 teaspoons Dijon-style mustard
3 tablespoons olive oil
   Fresh black pepper and salt to taste

Sherry Vinaigrette

•

1 tablespoon sherry vinegar, or: 1
   tablespoon wine vinegar mixed with
   1 teaspoon sherry
2 teaspoons Dijon-style mustard
3 tablespoons olive oil
   Fresh black pepper and salt to taste

Champagne Vinaigrette

•

1 tablespoon freshly squeezed lemon
   juice
1 tablespoon Champagne
2 teaspoons Dijon-style mustard
3 tablespoons olive oil
   Fresh black pepper and salt to taste

Lemon Vinaigrette

•

2 tablespoons freshly squeezed lemon
   juice
3 tablespoons olive oil
   Fresh black pepper and salt to taste

Walnut Vinaigrette

•

Proceed as for any of the above, but use wal-
nut or hazelnut oil instead of olive oil.

Although the thrust and emphasis of this book is on dinners, cholesterol (and caloric) awareness should be a three-meal concern. To observe an exemplary low-cholesterol dinner is both wise and good; but a wayward breakfast or lunch can undo all the good that the previous evening has wrought. Thus I offer some general and specific suggestions for breakfast, as well as ten luncheon menus to complement the gourmet dinners. Finally, the book includes a few cocktail-time recipes—often referred to as finger food—in keeping with the principles of this book, for I have observed that one of the most hazardous moments of the day is the cocktail hour.

Each menu is conceived for *four* people. However, many of my desserts serve as many as six or eight people, and in these cases—which are clearly marked —I suggest you put aside the additional servings for another meal. Each of the recipes—and menus—has been kitchen tested. They are followed by charts that give not only the cholesterol content per serving but the caloric, sodium, and saturated fat content, so that you can monitor those aspects of your diet as well. But bear in mind that the thrust of this book is on lowering dietary cholesterol levels.

It has been over a year since my husband and I began following this anti-cholesterol diet. Three months after we began, our tests showed that our levels had dropped appreciably. By the end of another three months we were both in the low-risk category. That translates into the comforting statistic that we have reduced our risk of heart attack to one-fourth of what it had been. Equally important, at least from our gourmet viewpoint, we have regaled ourselves in the process. If you have a cholesterol problem, but love good food, this book is for you.

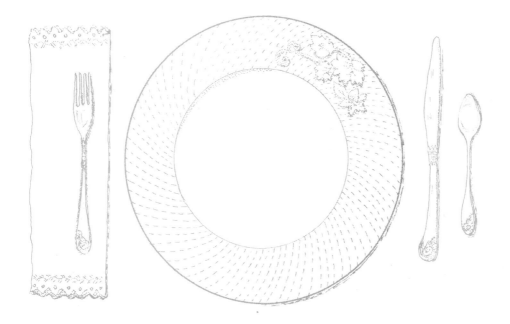

Dinners

$\mathscr{W}$hat follows is a selection of my favorite dinner menus. You may wish to cook them in their entirety or mix and match the recipes according to your own inspiration. Remember, all of these delicious dinners—which taste as sinfully good as some of the cholesterol-laden gastronomic feasts of yore—are in fact safe, light, and healthful. Although some of the menus are richer than others, they all fall within acceptable cholesterol parameters.

Menu 1

Mushrooms and Herbs in Filo Pastry
Roast Squab with Honey and Spices
Palette of Three Vegetable Purees
Sliced Oranges in Wine Syrup

Mushrooms and Herbs in Filo Pastry

I used to make this first course with puff pastry. Here I opt for filo dough, which is equally flaky but far less rich and cholesterol free. It should be noted that these individual mushroom pastries are a delightful appetizer, but they can serve as a luncheon course as well, accompanied by a green salad.

Juice of 1 lemon

½ pound button mushrooms, chopped fine

2 tablespoons olive oil, plus oil for brushing dough

2 medium onions, minced

1 cup finely chopped fresh parsley

½ cup minced fresh tarragon, or 1 tablespoon dried

Fresh pepper and salt to taste

16 sheets filo dough

1 teaspoon cornstarch

1 cup soy milk

Sprinkle lemon juice over mushrooms. In a skillet, heat 1 tablespoon oil, sauté half the onions until golden, add the mushrooms, and cook 5 minutes. Add half the parsley, plus the tarragon, pepper, and salt. Set aside.

Preheat the oven to 400°F. With a brush or a folded piece of absorbent paper, lightly oil one sheet of filo dough. Place a second sheet over the first and oil as well. Repeat for the third and fourth sheets, then fold the stack in half. Place roughly 2 tablespoons of the mushroom mixture in the center of the rectangle.

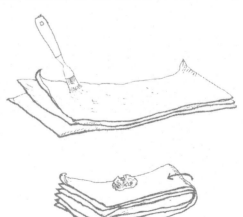

Fold the shorter sides over the filling, then turn and fold again into a small roll, so that the filling is completely enclosed. Repeat with the rest of the filo dough, until all the mushroom mixture is used. Brush lightly with oil, then place pastries, seam down, on a cookie sheet in a row. Bake for 20 minutes or until golden and fluffy.

In a saucepan, heat remaining tablespoon of oil and sauté remaining onions until golden. Add cornstarch and soy milk. Sprinkle with remaining parsley. Cook over low heat for 5 minutes until creamy. Transfer pastries onto individual small dinner plates, pour cream sauce over and around pastry, and serve.

Roast Squab with Honey and Spices

•

    4 squab, skins removed
    4 small cooking onions, left whole
    1 tablespoon dried tarragon
    ½ cup honey
    2 tablespoons Dijon-style mustard
    ½ cup fresh parsley, plus parsley for
        garnish
    ½ cup light soy sauce
    2 tablespoons olive oil

In each squab insert 1 onion, then sprinkle bird with 1 teaspoon tarragon. In a small bowl, combine the honey, remaining tarragon, mustard, parsley, and soy sauce.

Preheat the oven to 350°F. In a skillet, heat oil, reduce heat, and then brown squab on all sides. Transfer to an ovenproof dish, pour honey mixture over squab, and seal with foil. Bake for 45 minutes. Then sprinkle bird with

remaining tarragon. While the squab are baking, prepare your vegetables.

When squab are cooked, remove and place one on each plate. Use the purees to make a design resembling an artist's palette around each squab. Sprinkle with parsley and serve.

Palette of Three Vegetable Purees

•

For the red cabbage and beets

    1½ tablespoons olive oil
    1 onion, minced
    1 small red cabbage, shredded, then
        parboiled for 10 minutes and
        drained
    1 apple, peeled, cored, and diced
    1 teaspoon caraway seeds
    1 beet, peeled and boiled for 15
        minutes (not drained)
    1 tablespoon wine vinegar
    Fresh pepper to taste

In a large saucepan, heat oil and sauté onion until golden. Add cabbage, apple, caraway seeds, beet and beet juice, and vinegar. Reduce heat, cover, and cook for 30 minutes.

Transfer cabbage mixture to a blender or food processor and puree. Return to saucepan, add pepper and simmer over very low heat until ready to serve.

For the celery root

    1 large celery root, peeled and
        chopped
    2 small potatoes, peeled and cut in
        small pieces
    ½ cup 1% cottage cheese
    1 tablespoon olive oil
    Fresh pepper and salt to taste

Bring a quart of water to a boil in a large saucepan, drop in celery root and potatoes, reduce heat, and cook, covered, for 15 minutes. Drain. In a food processor or blender, combine cottage cheese, oil, and pepper and salt. Add celery and potatoes, and puree until smooth. Return to saucepan and simmer over very low heat until ready to serve.

For the broccoli

1 head broccoli, cut in florets, stemmed, peeled, and sliced

½ cup 1% cottage cheese

1 teaspoon grated nutmeg

Fresh pepper and salt to taste

In a large kettle, bring 1 quart of water to a boil. Add broccoli and cook for 8 minutes. Drain.

In a food processor or blender, puree broccoli, cottage cheese, nutmeg, pepper, and salt. Return to kettle and keep warm over very low heat until ready to serve.

Sliced Oranges in Wine Syrup

•

1 cup red wine (Beaujolais, or any red table wine)

½ cup sugar

1 tablespoon vanilla extract

4 seedless oranges, peeled and sliced

½ cup finely chopped dates

In a saucepan, bring the wine and sugar to a boil, reduce heat to low, and cook for 10 minutes, until mixture becomes syrupy. Add vanilla.

Place the oranges in a serving bowl, sprinkle on the dates, and pour on the wine syrup. Refrigerate for several hours. Serve cold.

	Calories	Cholesterol (mg)	Total Fat (g)	Saturated Fat (g)	Sodium (mg)
Mushrooms and Herbs in Filo Pastry	229	5	16	1	276
Roast Squab with Honey and Spices	368	90	15	3	1,492
Palette of Three Vegetable Purees	230	2	9	1	255
Sliced Oranges in Wine Syrup	220	0	0	0	0
TOTAL	1,047	97	40	5	2,023
% of Total Calories			34	4	

* Note: Quantities given indicate nutritional value per serving.

Menu

2

Blanquette of Halibut, Sorrel, Artichoke Hearts, and Potatoes

Endive and Walnut Salad

Strawberry Soufflé

This three-star menu is light and elegant, and with the exception of the soufflé (most of which can be prepared ahead of time), is easy to prepare.

Blanquette of Halibut, Sorrel, Artichoke Hearts, and Potatoes

•

12 small new potatoes, cut in halves
2 large artichokes
1 tablespoon olive oil
2 tablespoons minced shallots
1 pound fresh sorrel, coarsely chopped
1½ tablespoons unbleached all-purpose flour
Ground white pepper to taste
1½ cups skim milk
Juice of 1 lemon
1 cup finely chopped parsley
2 pounds boneless halibut, cut in 2-inch pieces

In a saucepan, cook potatoes in boiling water for 12 minutes. Drain and set aside. Cook artichokes for 20 minutes in boiling water. Drain, then remove leaves and choke. Cut hearts in 1-inch pieces. In a kettle, heat oil and sauté shallots until golden. Stir in sorrel and cook over low heat for 2 minutes. Add flour and pepper, and gradually stir in milk. Add lemon juice and parsley. Keep stirring until sauce is creamy smooth. Add the artichoke pieces and the potato halves, stir, and cook for 2 minutes. Add the fish, cover, and continue to cook over medium heat for 5 minutes. Serve.

Endive and Walnut Salad

•

3 to 4 Belgian endive, leaves separated
½ cup shelled walnuts
Sherry Vinaigrette (page xviii)

Place leaves in a large salad bowl. Sprinkle in walnuts and toss with vinaigrette.

Strawberry Soufflé

2 *pounds fresh strawberries, hulled*
⅔ *cup sugar*
  Juice of ½ lemon
1 *teaspoon kirsch*
2 *egg yolks (yes!)*
6 *egg whites, beaten until stiff*

Preheat the oven to 425°F. Lightly oil four individual soufflé dishes. In a food processor or blender, puree half the strawberries with half the sugar and the lemon juice, kirsch, and yolks. Very gently fold in the beaten whites, then pour mixture into soufflé dishes. (If there is any batter left, pour into an ovenproof dish for possible second helpings.)

Bake soufflés for 5 minutes at 425°F., then reduce oven temperature to 375°F. and continue baking for approximately 15 minutes more. Check to make sure the soufflés have risen above the rim of their dishes and have a rosy color. Serve with the strawberry sauce.

While soufflés bake, prepare the sauce. In a food processor or blender, puree the remaining strawberries with the remaining sugar. Pour sauce over soufflés and serve.

	Calories	Cholesterol (mg)	Total Fat (g)	Saturated Fat (g)	Sodium (mg)
Blanquette of Halibut, Sorrel, Artichoke Hearts, and Potatoes	720	121	10.5	1.0	206
Endive and Walnut Salad	201	—	22.5	—	1
Strawberry Soufflé	241	136	3.7	0.9	4
TOTAL	1,162	257	36.7	1.9	211
% of Total Calories			28	1	

* *Note:* Quantities given indicate nutritional value per serving.

Menu

3

Eggplant Crepes with Spinach Filling, on a Bed of Tomatoes with Red Pepper Vinaigrette

Grilled Breast of Chicken in Lime Marinade

Arugula Salad

Floating Islands Imperiale (sans yolks)

Eggplant Crepes with Spinach Filling on a Bed of Tomatoes Served with Red Pepper Vinaigrette

*E*ggplant is a wonderfully versatile vege-table, a perfect stand-in for countless foods, including meat. Note that in this book I make generous use of eggplant; in this recipe it replaces the crepe itself, which eliminates the flour, shortening, milk, and eggs in a standard crepe. In this menu I use the crepes as a first course, but for other occasions the eggplant crepes provide a perfect main course, followed by a salad.

For the crepes

2 tablespoons olive oil, approximately

1 large, wide eggplant, peeled and cut in thin, even slices

In a skillet over high heat, heat half a teaspoon of olive oil (enough to lubricate but not saturate the pan). Reduce heat to medium, and sauté

eggplant slices on both sides until translucent to light brown, adding a few drops of oil as needed. Remove eggplant slices onto absorbent paper to drain and set aside. Repeat until all the eggplant is cooked.

For the tomato bed

1 tablespoon olive oil

1 large onion, minced

1 garlic clove, minced

4 large tomatoes, peeled and cubed

1 handful of fresh basil, chopped, or 1 teaspoon dried

A few sprigs of fresh thyme, or ½ teaspoon dried

A few fresh oregano leaves, or 1 teaspoon dried

Fresh pepper to taste

In a skillet, heat the oil and sauté the onion and garlic for the tomato bed until translucent. Add the tomatoes and herbs, then cook for 5 to 8 minutes. Set aside.

For the spinach filling

1 (10-ounce) package frozen chopped
  spinach
4 ounces 1 percent cottage cheese
½ teaspoon grated nutmeg

Cook the spinach for the filling according to directions on the package, then drain thoroughly by pressing firmly with a fork in a colander. In a food processor or blender puree the spinach, cottage cheese, and nutmeg; or mix ingredients by hand with a fork in a bowl.

To roast peppers, hold them over a medium flame on top of a gas stove and char, or until skins are blackened and cracked. (If you do not have access to a gas stove, bake in oven at 350°F. for 15 minutes until skins crack.) Under cold running water peel the peppers, ridding them of the blackened skin. Remove seeds, then puree flesh in a blender or food processor. Add oil, vinegar, and pepper, and stir until well blended. Set aside.

Preheat the oven to 300°F. Lightly coat a large ovenproof dish with a bit of olive oil. Spread an eggplant slice with a tablespoon of the spinach filling, then roll slice lengthwise into a cylinder. Place in baking dish. Repeat until all slices are used, then cover dish and heat for 15 minutes.

For the red pepper vinaigrette

3 red bell peppers
3 tablespoons olive oil
1 tablespoon balsamic vinegar
  Fresh pepper to taste

On each plate, spread 2 or 3 tablespoons of the tomato mixture. Then put 2 crepes on each plate and trickle over 2 to 3 teaspoons of the red pepper vinaigrette. Serve at once.

Grilled Breast of Chicken in Lime Marinade

•

½ cup chopped fresh coriander
  (cilantro)
  Juice of 2 limes
1 shallot, minced
½ teaspoon ground pepper
4 whole chicken breasts, skin off·

In a blender, liquefy the coriander, lime juice, shallot, and pepper. Place chicken breasts in a noncorrosive bowl and pour in marinade. Cover and refrigerate for at least 30 minutes. (You may do this the night before.)

Prepare a grill and cook breasts for 8 to 10 minutes on each side, basting with marinade. (If you don't have a grill, you can use a ridged pan to cook breasts on top of the stove.) When both sides are nicely grilled, serve.

Arugula Salad

•

*S*ince the first course of this menu is rather substantial, I suggest serving salad only, either with the chicken or after.

2 bunches arugula
  Sherry Vinaigrette (page xviii)

Wash arugula thoroughly and dry. Stem leaves, then toss with vinaigrette.

Floating Islands Imperiale (Sans Yolk)

•

*T*his is one of the most traditional French desserts. The problem is, from a cholesterol viewpoint, it is strictly forbidden. Why? Because this exquisite dessert is laden with egg yolks and cream. After much experimenting, however, I created a vanilla custard cream that is completely cholesterol free. For taste and texture, this vanilla cream could pass for the original.

For the custard and meringues

- 2 tablespoons polyunsaturated margarine
- 2 tablespoons cornstarch
- 3½ cups vanilla soy milk
- 2 tablespoons vanilla extract
- ½ cup granulated sugar
- 1 tablespoon confectioners' sugar
- 3 egg whites, beaten until stiff

Melt margarine in a 1-quart saucepan, add cornstarch, and gradually stir in soy milk until mixture becomes thick but is still liquid. Add the vanilla. Pour custard cream into a large serving bowl and refrigerate.

Preheat the oven to 200°F. Fold both sugars into the beaten whites. On a cookie sheet covered with a sheet of foil, drop spoonfuls of the egg-white mixture to form little mounds. Bake for about 1½ hours, or until the meringues are dry and crisp yet still white. Turn off oven and leave meringues in oven, with door open. When meringues are cool, lift off the foil sheet with a spatula and place atop custard cream. Put bowl back in refrigerator until ready to serve.

To serve

- ½ cup fresh raspberries
- ½ cup granulated sugar

Remove custard cream from refrigerator and add the raspberries before preparing the angel hair.

In a medium saucepan set over medium heat, melt sugar until it turns amber. Turn off heat and stir with a wooden spoon. When caramel thickens and cools a bit, pull upward with the spoon, creating caramel threads. (This step is a little tricky, since the caramel can cool too much to make proper angel hair. If that happens, warm over low heat until caramel liquefies a little, then proceed.) Cover meringues with caramel threads—angel hair—creating a nest effect. Serve at once.

	Calories	Cholesterol (mg)	Total Fat (g)	Saturated Fat (g)	Sodium (mg)
Eggplant Crepes with Spinach Filling	236	1	15.5	2.1	196
Grilled Breast of Chicken—Lime Marinade	177	85	4.5	1.3	77
Arugula Salad	35	—	2	—	300
Floating Islands Imperiale	330	—	8.7	1.0	123
TOTAL	778	86	30.7	4.4	696
% of Total Calories			36	5	

* *Note:* Quantities given indicate nutritional value per serving.

Menu

4

**Bouillabaisse of Vegetables
with Garlic Toast and My Rouille**

Boston Lettuce Salad

Warm Plum Tart

Bouillabaisse of Vegetables

*T*his attractive and healthful course is a meal in itself. Like the original bouilla-baisse, it combines soup and entrée in one course. Those I have served it to have found it as exotic and satisfying as its better-known Mediterranean fish equivalent.

2 tablespoons olive oil

2 medium-size onions, chopped

1 medium-size zucchini, cut in fourths lengthwise

4 garlic cloves whole, peeled

½ teaspoon (a few shreds) saffron

½ cup fresh basil leaves

1 cup finely chopped fresh parsley

½ teaspoon dried thyme

½ teaspoon dried oregano

2 tablespoons tomato paste

3 cups dry white wine

3 cups water

8 carrots, peeled

4 potatoes, peeled and halved

4 to 6 celery stalks, peeled

1 fennel bulb, cut in fourths

1 head broccoli, separated into florets

4 tomatoes, peeled and halved

Fresh pepper and salt to taste

Garlic toast (recipe follows)

Rouille (recipe follows)

In a large kettle, heat the oil and sauté the onions until golden. Add the garlic, saffron, basil, parsley, thyme, oregano, tomato paste, wine, water, carrots, and potatoes. Stir well and cover. Cook over medium heat for 8 minutes, then add the celery and fennel and continue cooking for another 8 minutes. Add the broccoli and tomatoes, then cook for an additional 4 minutes. Season with salt and pepper to taste. Serve.

Garlic Toast

*I*t is traditional and mandatory to serve garlic toast with bouillabaisse. In France, the toast is made from slices of baguette. In the event a baguette is not available, whole wheat toast is a satisfactory equivalent.

> *⅓ cup olive oil*
> *12 slices baguette (French bread), or 6 slices whole wheat bread, cut in half*
> *3 garlic cloves, minced*

In a skillet, heat oil and add bread. When one side is golden brown, turn bread over and spread garlic on the browned side. Continue cooking until both sides are done. Drain on absorbent paper and set aside until ready to serve.

My Rouille

*T*he traditional rouille, of course, is rich with egg yolks. Mine, which is cholesterol free, rivals the original in both taste and effect.

> *4 slices whole wheat bread, soaked in water and squeezed dry*
> *8 garlic cloves, peeled*

> *1 tablespoon tomato paste*
> *1 tablespoon water*
> *¾ cup olive oil*
> *¾ cup tomato juice*
> *1 teaspoon cayenne pepper*
> *½ cup chopped fresh parsley*

In a food processor or blender, puree the bread, garlic, tomato paste, and water. While the processor is still turning, trickle in the olive oil slowly from the top, until you obtain a mayonnaise consistency. Add the cayenne pepper and parsley.

Stir 2 tablespoons of the rouille into the bouillabaisse. To serve, bring kettle directly to the table. Place one piece of each vegetable into individual soup plates, then ladle over some soup liquid. Place 2 to 3 garlic toasts around the plates, and top with a dollop of rouille. Pass the bowl of rouille for additional servings.

Boston Lettuce Salad

> *1 head Boston lettuce*
> *Vinaigrette of your choice (page xviii)*

Wash and dry lettuce leaves. Tear into bite-size pieces and dress with vinaigrette.

The (Almost) No Cholesterol Gourmet Cookbook

Warm Plum Tart

3 *ounces low-fat cream cheese*

12 *tablespoons polyunsaturated margarine*

1 *cup unbleached all-purpose flour*

1 *cup wheat bran*

½ *cup rolled oats*

2 *pounds plums, pitted and halved*

½ *cup brown sugar, either light or dark*

1 *tablespoon vanilla extract*

½ *cup plum jam*

⅓ *cup plum brandy*

Preheat the oven to 375°F.

In a bowl or food processor, blend the cream cheese, margarine (reserving 1 tablespoon), flour, bran, and oats to form a smooth dough. Wrap and refrigerate for 30 minutes.

Roll out dough and place in an 8-inch pie pan. Prick all over with a fork and bake for 15 minutes. Remove from oven and place plums, skin side down, to cover dough. You may overlap if need be. Sprinkle half the brown sugar over the plums along with the vanilla. Dot with remaining tablespoon of margarine. Bake for 20 minutes. Remove from oven and cool for 15 minutes.

In a small saucepan over low heat, heat jam with the remaining brown sugar, and stir for 2 minutes with a wooden spoon until it thickens. Stir in brandy and cook for a few additional seconds, stirring well. Pour glaze evenly over top to cover plums. Serve warm. (*Serves 8.*)

	Calories	Cholesterol (mg)	Total Fat (g)	Saturated Fat (g)	Sodium (mg)
Bouillabaisse of Vegetables	510	—	7.0	0.9	482
Garlic Toast	263	—	18.0	2.4	225
Rouille	440	—	40.5	5.4	290
Boston Lettuce Salad	98	—	10.3	1.4	2
Warm Plum Tart	449	6	20.0	4.0	208
TOTAL	1,760	—	95.8	14.1	1,207
% of Total Calories			49	7	

* *Note:* Quantities given indicate nutritional value per serving.

Menu

5

Nouvelle Gnocchi with Marsala, Tomato, Mushrooms, and Breast of Chicken

Watercress Salad

Raspberry Tart

Nouvelle Gnocchi with Marsala, Tomato, Mushrooms, and Breast of Chicken

*

By tradition, good gnocchi must be rich yet very light. The primary ingredient is several large eggs. In the sauce are usually cream and Parmesan cheese, topped with butter, more cream, and more Parmesan cheese. In other words, it's deadly but oh so good!

My recipe is as light as the classic and just as tasty, but it contains no egg yolks, no cheese, no cream, and no butter. Epicures who might frown at the loss of those elements should be reassured: I have served these gnocchi to gourmets and they have raved about the dish. Some of the more health-conscious guests hinted at the legendary high cholesterol, at which point I revealed the truth.

For the gnocchi

1 cup water

6 tablespoons polyunsaturated margarine

1 cup unbleached all-purpose flour, semolina, or farina

6 egg whites

1 teaspoon freshly grated nutmeg
Salt

In a saucepan, heat water and margarine until margarine is melted. Drop in flour all at once. Turn off heat and stir vigorously. When flour and water are well mixed, add egg whites and nutmeg, and stir constantly until mixture becomes a puttylike paste. It takes a little work for the mixture to become well integrated— perhaps up to 5 minutes; if you have a food processor, you can do this step in 1 minute.

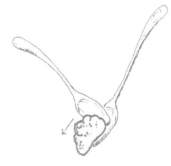

In a 4-quart kettle, preferably with a wide rim, bring 2 quarts of water to a boil with a teaspoon of salt. Using 2 teaspoons as your tools (one to scoop and one to ease the paste into the boiling water), drop 1 teaspoon of the paste into the water. Repeat until pot is filled. Do not overfill; you may need to do this in two or even three batches, depending on the width of your pot. Reduce heat to a simmer. The gnocchi will first drop to the bottom, then rise to the surface one by one. Allow gnocchi to continue simmering for 1 to 2 minutes, then with a slotted spoon, gently remove them and set aside on a platter.

For the Marsala, Tomato, Mushrooms, and Breast of Chicken

    4 tablespoons olive oil
    1 large onion, finely chopped
    2 cups boneless breast of chicken,
      skins removed, cut into strips
    6 to 8 mushrooms, sliced and
      julienned
    2 garlic cloves, whole
    1 cup finely chopped fresh parsley
      Few leaves of fresh sage, minced
      (optional)
      Pepper and salt
    3 teaspoons cornstarch
    1 cup skim milk

    2 tablespoons tomato paste
    4 tomatoes, sliced and julienned
    ½ teaspoon freshly grated nutmeg
    ¼ cup Marsala wine
    2 tablespoons bran
    2 tablespoons wheat germ

In a large saucepan heat the oil, sauté onions until golden brown, add chicken, and cook for 8 minutes, stirring. Add mushrooms, garlic, parsley, sage, pepper, and salt. In a cup mix cornstarch with skim milk and tomato paste. Stir into pot and cook for 3 minutes, adding a little water if it thickens too much. Add tomatoes, cook 2 minutes, stirring. Season with nutmeg and Marsala. Gently fold in the gnocchi. Transfer to an ovenproof dish. Top with bran and wheat germ. Dot with a few drops of olive oil (or dots of margarine). If you are serving immediately, put under broiler for 2 to 3 minutes until top gets brown and crispy. (If you make it in advance, refrigerate the dish and reheat it in an oven preheated to 350°F. for 15 to 20 minutes.)

Note: The bran and wheat germ, in addition to being healthy, are a friendly facsimile to the missing Parmesan.

Watercress Salad

•

The crispness of the watercress complements the gnocchi main course nicely. Arugula will do nicely too, but is not always available everywhere.

    1 bunch watercress
      Vinaigrette or your choice (page
      xviii)

Wash and trim watercress. Dress with vinaigrette.

Raspberry Tart

•

For the crust

8 tablespoons polyunsaturated
  margarine
3 ounces 1% cottage cheese
1½ cups unbleached flour
2 ice cubes

In a food processor, put margarine, cottage cheese, flour, and ice cubes. Mix for a minute or two until dough is formed. Remove, wrap, and refrigerate for 30 minutes. Preheat oven to 350°F. Roll out dough, place in 8 to 10 inch pie mold, and bake for 20 minutes until golden. Remove. Let cool.

For the Filling

1 pint raspberries, washed
4 tablespoons raspberry jam
2 teaspoons sugar

When pie crust has cooled, transfer to serving platter. Fill evenly with raspberries. In a small saucepan, melt the jam with the sugar, stirring for about 1 minute. Coat raspberries with this glaze.

Note: If your jam has a lot of seeds, press it through a little sieve as you glaze.

	Calories	Cholesterol (mg)	Total Fat (g)	Saturated Fat (g)	Sodium (mg)
Nouvelle Gnocchi with Marsala, Tomato, Mushrooms, and Breast of Chicken	695	84	39	6.9	752
Watercress Salad	100	—	10.5	5.4	638
Raspberry Tart	232	0.5	11.7	2.1	139
TOTAL	1,027	85	61.2	14.4	1,529
% of Total Calories			54	13	

* *Note:* Quantities given indicate nutritional value per serving.

Poached Leeks Mimosa in Sherry Vinaigrette

Chicken Kiev Remembered...

Steamed Rice

Gratin of Pears and Almonds

Poached Leeks Mimosa in Sherry Vinaigrette

·

This is one of France's traditional hors d'oeuvres, a wonderful alternative to *asparagus vinaigrette*. "Mimosa" refers to hard-boiled eggs that have been finely chopped and sprinkled over the vegetable. Tailoring the concept to our needs, I use only the whites, which, when combined with chopped parsley, are as good as the original.

4 large leeks, green part cut off and white part sliced lengthwise
Salt to taste
1 cup finely chopped fresh parsley
4 hard-boiled egg whites, finely chopped

Fresh pepper to taste
Sherry Vinaigrette (page xviii)

Leeks, like fresh spinach, contain a fair amount of sand and must be washed very thoroughly. To make sure you've got rid of all the sand, make several cuts lengthwise in the leeks and soak them in a bowl of water, changing the water several times as needed.

In a kettle, bring 1 quart of water to a boil. Add a pinch of salt and cook the leeks over medium heat for 10 to 15 minutes. Drain and allow to cool. Portion out the leeks onto individual plates and sprinkle liberally with parsley and egg whites. Season to taste with pepper. Pour the vinaigrette on each serving.

Chicken Kiev Remembered ...

*T*he fun of chicken Kiev is in the surprise of seeing butter spurt out at the first cut of the knife. We retain the full effect while making the dish cholesterol safe.

For the filling

2 tablespoons polyunsaturated margarine

2 ounces 1% cottage cheese

2 tablespoons minced scallions

2 tablespoons finely chopped fresh parsley

2 tablespoons fresh tarragon, or 1 tablespoon dried

1 tablespoon fresh lemon juice

For the chicken

4 half chicken breasts, skinned and boned, and flattened with a rolling pin or a meat pounder

½ cup whole wheat flour

3 egg whites, lightly beaten with 2 tablespoons water and 1 teaspoon olive oil

1 cup wheat germ

1 cup bran cereal, ground

1 cup bread crumbs

1 cup peanut oil, for frying

In a food processor or a mixing bowl with a fork, combine the filling ingredients. Form a rectangle, place between 2 sheets of foil or paper, and refrigerate for 30 minutes. When well chilled, remove from refrigerator and divide rectangle into 4 equal parts. Place a filling on the wider side of the chicken breast, then fold over the smaller side, making sure the chicken "package" is well sealed. (Poultry pins or wooden toothpicks may further secure the fold.) Repeat for remaining 3 breasts. Refrigerate for at least 10 minutes.

Meanwhile, place 3 soup plates side by side on your kitchen table. In one, put the flour; in the second put the egg-white mixture; in the third, put the wheat germ, cereal, and bread crumbs. Coat the chicken packages first with the flour, then the egg-white mixture, and finally the crumbs. Refrigerate for 1 hour. (Recipe may be done up to this point the day before.)

In a deep kettle, heat the oil and fry the chicken packages for 8 to 10 minutes, turning them until all sides are golden and crisp. Drain well on paper towel. Serve.

Steamed Rice

*C*ook your favorite rice, following the directions on the box. I highly recommend Indian basmati rice—either white or brown.

Gratin of Pears and Almonds

*T*his is a delectable gratin I've often made in the past with a zabaglione base, which contains egg yolks. My alternative now is just as delicious and is also cholesterol safe. Any variety of good eating pear available at your local produce market will do fine in this dessert.

6 ripe pears, peeled, cored, and
  sliced
Juice of ½ lemon

½ cup slivered almonds
1 teaspoon almond extract
3 egg whites, beaten until stiff and
  combined with ⅓ cup sugar

Preheat the broiler. In 4 individual broiler-proof dishes (or 1 large dish), place pear slices side by side. Pour lemon juice over, then sprinkle on the almonds and extract. Top with the egg-white mixture. Place under broiler for 8 to 10 minutes, or until top turns light brown. Serve.

	Calories	Cholesterol (mg)	Total Fat (g)	Saturated Fat (g)	Sodium (mg)
Poached Leeks Mimosa in Sherry Vinaigrette	251	—	14.0	1.8	341
Chicken Kiev Remembered . . .	654	74.0	28.0	5.2	518
Steamed Rice	110	—	—	—	5
Gratin of Pears and Almonds	319	—	9.0	0.8	2
TOTAL	1,334	74.0	51.0	7.8	866
% of Total Calories			34	5	

* *Note:* Quantities given indicate nutritional value per serving.

Couscous of Halibut and Salmon

Green Apple Sorbet on a Green Apple Fan

Couscous of Halibut and Salmon

•

*C*ouscous, like gazpacho in Spain, appears in variations throughout North Africa, the constants being only the cereal and hot sauce. The classic dish features lamb, chicken, or fish; this low-cholesterol version calls for grilled fish. I have also opted to serve the vegetables diced and already integrated into the cereal, rather than as part of the sauce.

2 tablespoons olive oil
1 onion, finely chopped
1 turnip, peeled and diced
1 carrot, peeled and diced
1 red bell pepper, diced
1 zucchini, diced
2 cups quick-cooking couscous

2 cups water
2 cups chick peas, cooked
1 cup finely chopped fresh coriander (cilantro), (optional)
½ cup honey
2 tablespoons light soy sauce
  Juice of 1 lemon
1 teaspoon ground cumin
1 teaspoon hot paprika
2 cups peanut oil, for deep-frying
2 leeks, washed well, trimmed (discard the very dark green portion), and cut in threadlike strips
2 halibut steaks, about ¼ pound each
2 salmon steaks, about ¼ pound each
1 cup finely chopped fresh parsley

There are 3 steps to making this couscous, excluding the grilling of the fish: (1) make the sauce, (2) deep-fry the leeks, and (3) prepare the vegetables and cereal. While the list of ingredients and number of steps may imply a discouragingly complex recipe, do not be deterred; this dish is relatively easy and not overly long to prepare.

For the vegetables and cereal

In a kettle, heat the olive oil and sauté the onion until golden brown. Stir in the turnip and carrot, and cook for 3 minutes. Stir in the red pepper and zucchini, and cook for an additional 3 minutes.

Stir in the couscous, add the water, bring to a boil, turn off heat, then stir vigorously until ingredients are well integrated and fluffy. Add the chick peas and cover. Let sit for 5 minutes, then add the coriander.

For the sauce

In a small saucepan over low heat, combine the honey, soy sauce, lemon juice, cumin, and paprika. Cook 5 minutes, then set aside.

For the leeks

In a large saucepan, heat the peanut oil until it sizzles when you drop in a tiny piece of leek. Pat-dry the leek threads and deep-fry for about 10 minutes, or until they are crisp. Drain well on absorbent paper and set aside. You have now made the angel hair of leeks.

For the fish

Grill or broil the fish steaks for 5 minutes on each side.

On a large platter, spread the cereal mixture, then arrange the fish steaks on top. Pour the honey sauce equally over each fish and decorate with the angel of leeks and parsley. Serve.

Green Apple Sorbet
on a Green Apple Fan

*T*he cholesterol-reducing qualities of apples are well documented. Here we take one virtue and double it, at the same time adding a light touch of elegance. After the very substantial and spicy couscous, this cool, refreshing dessert is a welcome conclusion to the meal.

For the sorbet

1 cup water

⅓ cup granulated sugar

5 Granny Smith apples, peeled, cored, and cut in fourths

½ cup lemon juice

⅓ cup confectioners' sugar

2 egg whites, beaten until stiff

For the fan

2 Granny Smith apples, cored and thinly sliced

Juice of ½ lemon

¼ cup Calvados (optional)

In a saucepan, combine water and granulated sugar. Cook over medium heat for 10 to 15 minutes, or until liquid thickens to a syrup. Chill. In a food processor or blender, puree the apples and lemon juice, trickling in the sugar syrup. Pour into a metallic bowl and freeze for 30 minutes.

In a separate bowl, fold confectioners' sugar into the beaten whites. Place bowl in a pan of boiling water and heat for 10 minutes, until mixture becomes satiny. Remove from water and place in freezer. Freeze for 30 minutes.

Combine contents of both bowls with a spoon or fork until thoroughly mixed. Freeze for at least 2 hours. (This is the old-fashioned method of making sorbet without a machine. If you have an ice-cream maker, follow the manufacturer's instructions after making the syrup and puree.)

Make a fan of apple slices on 4 dessert plates, to cover about one third of each plate. Sprinkle with the lemon juice. At the base of each fan, place 1 or 2 scoops of sorbet, and splash with a bit of Calvados. Serve.

	Calories	Cholesterol (mg)	Total Fat (g)	Saturated Fat (g)	Sodium (mg)
Couscous of Halibut and Salmon	1,327	85	66.1	10.1	370
Green Apple Sorbet on a Green Apple Fan	208	—	—	—	25
TOTAL	1,535	85	66.1	10.1	395
% of Total Calories			39	6	

* *Note:* Quantities given indicate nutritional value per serving.

Menu

8

Brandied Bisque of Mussels

Sea Scallops in a Triangle of Leeks

New Potatoes

**Boston Lettuce in a Champagne and
Lemon Vinaigrette**

Macédoine of Fresh Fruit

Hazelnut Macaroons

Brandied Bisque of Mussels

*T*he terms *bisque* conjures up images of a thick seafood soup made with cream, butter, and yolks—therefore anathema to the present context. But that does not mean you need to eliminate bisque from your vocabulary or repertoire. Here is a rich, creamy bisque without an egg yolk or even a trace of cream or butter.

    4 to 5 pounds mussels
¼ cup cornmeal
    2 cups dry white wine
    2 onions, minced
½ cup finely chopped fresh parsley
    1 bay leaf

    1 teaspoon dried thyme
    3 tablespoons olive oil
    Fresh pepper and salt to taste
    2 tablespoons potato starch
    1 quart soy milk
¼ cup brandy
    Juice of 1 lemon

Scrub the mussels well under running water, removing the beard. Soak in several changes of water. To the last of these add the cornmeal; this causes the mussels to expel any sand. Let soak for 1 hour.

    Remove mussels from water, rinse again, and place in a large kettle, with 1 cup of the wine, half the onions and parsley, the bay leaf, and the thyme. Cover, bring to a boil, reduce heat, and cook for 4 to 5 minutes. (Shake the kettle several times to evenly distribute the steam.) When the mussels are open, they are done. Discard any that remain closed.

Over a bowl, drain mussels through a colander. Strain mussel liquid through several layers of cheesecloth into a measuring cup. Add remaining 1 cup wine and enough water to make 4 cups liquid. Set aside.

Remove most mussels from their shells, setting aside a dozen in their shells for later use as decoration. In a large kettle, heat the oil and sauté the remaining onion until golden. Add the salt and pepper and the potato starch, stir in mussel liquid, and gradually add the soy milk. Stir in the mussels and parsley, then cook over low heat for 5 to 8 minutes.

While the soup simmers, remove half the mussels and quickly puree in a blender with a cup or so of the soup. Return the pureed mussels to kettle and stir. Adjust seasoning and add brandy and lemon juice. Five minutes prior to serving, add reserved mussels in their shells. Serve piping hot.

Sea Scallops in a Triangle of Leeks

*

*T*his delicate and light recipe seems especially suited to this new regime. I often substitute flounder for scallops. And when I serve it as a main course, I offer four or five triangles per person; as an hors d'oeuvre, one or two suffice.

2 leeks, preferably wide, with greens cut off
20 to 25 sea scallops (or 2 flounder filets, cut in 1-inch pieces, about ½ pound)
Juice of 1 lemon
½ cup finely chopped fresh dill, or 1½ tablespoons dried
1 cup finely chopped fresh parsley
Fresh pepper to taste
2 tablespoons olive oil

Separate the layers of the bulbous portion of the leeks and wash thoroughly (like spinach, leeks tend to be sandy). In a kettle, bring 1 quart of water to a boil. Immerse the leeks and blanch for 5 minutes. Drain. Place leeks on absorbent paper and pat dry.

In a bowl, marinate the scallops (or fish pieces) in the lemon juice, dill, half the parsley, and the pepper for at least 10 minutes.

If the leek is wide enough, place 1 scallop in the center and fold 3 corners into a triangle. If the leek is narrow, use 2 overlapping leek leaves and proceed as above. Repeat until all scallops are used.

Preheat the oven to 300°F. In a skillet, heat the oil and sauté the triangles over medium heat, turning them with a spatula until golden on both sides. Place in an ovenproof dish, cover, and keep warm in oven until ready to serve.

New Potatoes

•

12 new potatoes, medium size,
     unpeeled and scrubbed
½ cup finely chopped fresh parsley
½ cup finely chopped fresh dill
½ tablespoon olive oil
     Fresh pepper and salt

In a large saucepan, cover potatoes with water
and cook for about 12 to 15 minutes. Drain.
Place potatoes back in saucepan, heat for 1
minute, then sprinkle with parsley, dill, and
olive oil. Season to taste and serve.

Boston Lettuce in a Champagne and Lemon Vinaigrette

•

*T*his is a lovely variation on an otherwise
classic salad dressing, which I serve
when I have some Champagne left over after a
party.

1 head Boston lettuce
1 tablespoon Champagne
   Juice of ½ lemon
1 teaspoon dried tarragon
1 tablespoon Dijon-style mustard
3 tablespoons virgin olive oil
   Fresh pepper and salt to taste

Separate the leaves of a firm and pale Boston
lettuce. Wash and dry, add Champagne vinaigrette, toss, and serve.

Macédoine of Fresh Fruit

•

1 ripe peach, peeled and diced
10 fresh strawberries, hulled and
     sliced (or frozen, if fresh
     unavailable)
½ cup fresh raspberries (or frozen, if
     fresh unavailable)
½ cup seedless grapes
1 pear, peeled and diced
1 orange, peeled and sliced
½ cup pitted and diced dates
½ cup orange juice
1 tablespoon sugar
¼ cup orange brandy or rum
     (optional)

In a serving bowl, combine all the ingredients,
chill for several hours, and serve.

Hazelnut Macaroons

•

2 cups hazelnuts, ground
⅔ cup sugar
1 teaspoon almond extract
2 egg whites

Preheat the oven to 350°F. In a mixing bowl,
combine all the above ingredients to form a
sticky paste. Use a tablespoon or your hands,
to form mounds roughly the size of a Ping-
Pong ball and place them 2 inches apart on a
greased cookie sheet. Bake for 20 minutes.
(*Serve 8.*)

Note: Macaroons should be nicely chewy,
which is why you should not bake them for
more than 20 minutes.

	Calories	Cholesterol (mg)	Total Fat (g)	Saturated Fat (g)	Sodium (mg)
Brandied Bisque of Mussels	347	32	13.0	0.9	629
Scallops in a Triangle of Leeks	182	18	7.2	1.6	95
New Potatoes	90	—	—	—	250
Boston Lettuce in a Champagne and Lemon Vinaigrette	101	—	10.2	1.4	115
Macédoine of Fresh Fruit	125	—	—	—	—
Hazelnut Macaroons	204	—	13.5	1.0	2
TOTAL	1,049	50	43.9	4.9	1,091
% of Total Calories			43	2	

* *Note:* Quantities given indicate nutritional value per serving.

Menu

9

Mosaic of Vegetables
with a Red Pepper and Tomato Coulis

Chicken in a Salt Crust

Steamed Carrots, New Potatoes, and Leeks
with Two Sauces

Poached Plums and Peaches,
with Fresh Blueberries and Strawberries

This is a grand menu in all senses of the term, not only for its low cholesterol, but also because it is ultralight. At the same time, its attractive and dramatic appearance creates a festive mood worthy of any gala occasion. The mosaic of vegetables, with its multitude of colors, shines in a lemon aspic. The main course is concealed in a crust that you open dramatically at the moment of serving, to reveal the sight and aroma of a steamed chicken.

The vegetables are served on a separate platter, accompanied by two contrasting sauces: one horseradish, the other watercress. The dessert offers a colorful and unusual mixture of poached and fresh fruit.

Mosaic of Vegetables with a Red Pepper and Tomato Coulis

Unlike most recipes in this book, this does require a bit of time, because there are a number of steps involved and a

goodly number of ingredients. It's a dish I enjoy preparing during a weekend, when I have more time. It's a fairly easy recipe and the results are well worth the effort.

For the terrine

4 carrots, peeled and sliced

4 turnips, peeled and sliced

¼ pound green beans, trimmed

1 zucchini, trimmed and sliced

¼ pound asparagus, peeled and trimmed

Salt and fresh pepper

5 (1-ounce) package unflavored gelatin

Juice of 1 lemon

5 cups cold water

2 artichokes, cooked, with leaves discarded and hearts sliced

½ cup finely chopped fresh basil

For the coulis

2 *tablespoons olive oil*

1 *onion, minced*

1 *tomato, cubed*

1 *red bell pepper, roasted and peeled*

1 *celery stalk, peeled and diced*

½ *cup finely chopped fresh parsley*

1 *teaspoon dried thyme*

½ *teaspoon ground bay leaf*

Fresh pepper and salt to taste

1 *tablespoon wine vinegar*

Chopped fresh parsley, for top

Cook the carrots, turnips, beans, zucchini, and asparagus separately—in individual pots—then drain on absorbent paper and set aside. Recommended times for tender-crisp vegetables are as follows, from the time the water boils: carrots and turnips, 5 to 8 minutes each; green beans, 4 minutes (refresh beans under cold water before draining); asparagus, 5 minutes; zucchini, 2 minutes. Lightly salt and pepper vegetables to taste.

In a bowl, dissolve gelatin in lemon juice and ½ cup cold water. Add 4 additional cups water, then bring to a boil, stirring constantly. Turn off heat and let gelatin cool to syrupy consistency, about 30 to 40 minutes.

In an oblong dish or 9 × 5-inch loaf pan, pour 1 cup of the cooled gelatin. Place asparagus in the gelatin and refrigerate for 15 minutes. Remove pan from refrigerator and pour in another half-cup of gelatin, then top with the carrot slices; refrigerate for 5 to 10 minutes. Repeat process several times, adding gelatin and turnips, gelatin and zucchini, gelatin and artichoke hearts, gelatin and beans. Cover bean layer with final ½ cup of gelatin, topped with basil. Refrigerate a minimum of 4 to 5 hours.

To make the coulis, heat the oil in a skillet and sauté the onion until golden. Add tomato, red pepper, celery, parsley, thyme, and bay leaf. Cook for 10 minutes, then add pepper and salt to taste. Puree contents of skillet in a food processor or blender, adding vinegar. Refrigerate.

When ready to serve, place terrine in a pan of hot water for a few seconds. Run a knife around edges, then place serving platter on top and invert. Pour roughly half the coulis around the terrine; pour remainder in a serving bowl to pass at the table. Sprinkle parsley over coulis. At table, slice terrine as you would a pâté. (As an alternative, remove terrine from pan, slice into portions, and place on individual dishes that already have been lightly spread with coulis.)

Chicken in a Salt Crust

*T*he salt crust is not edible; it is merely meant for baking, and should be discarded. (Because the chicken is prepared with absolutely no fat or liquid, and it cooks in its own steam, I like to flavor it with a sprig or two of rosemary and tarragon and a few slices of lime, but you may prefer other herbs.) Unlike other recipes in this book, this cooks the chicken with the skin on. But because of the method used, the skin is easily removed at the time of serving.

8 *cups unbleached all-purpose flour*
4 *cups salt*
7 *tablespoons water*
1 *chicken, about 4 to 5 pounds*
1 *medium onion, peeled and whole*
  Peel of 1 lime, cut into strips
1 *sprig of rosemary*
1 *sprig of tarragon*

Preheat the oven to 375°F. Place the flour, salt, and water in a large mixing bowl. Use your hands to form a smooth dough, then turn out onto a floured board. Roll dough into a rectangle more than twice the length and width of your chicken.

Rinse chicken and pat dry. Insert the onion and some of the lime strips into the cavity. Place chicken in the center of the dough. Put the rosemary and tarragon sprigs, plus remaining lime strips, on top of chicken. Wrap the chicken with the dough, sealing it tightly by pinching the ends closed. Place dough-wrapped chicken on a cookie sheet or in a baking dish and bake for 1½ hours. The crust should become rock-hard.

Remove chicken from oven. Place on a large platter and bring to the table. Your theatrical moment is about to begin. With a solid carving knife—serrated, if possible—carve off the top of the crust. Lift chicken out, onto a serving platter. Remove skin and carve chicken. Serve hot.

Steamed Carrots, New Potatoes and Leeks with Two Sauces

For the vegetables

9 *to 10 small new potatoes, scrubbed, unpeeled and whole*
8 *carrots, peeled and left whole*
4 *thin leeks, trimmed, or 1 thick leek, cut lengthwise*

For the horseradish sauce

½ *cup prepared horseradish*
½ *cup 1% cottage cheese*

For the watercress sauce

2 *cups water*
1 *bunch watercress, chopped*
½ *cup 1% cottage cheese*

Twenty minutes before the chicken is done, steam the vegetables for 12 to 18 minutes, depending on how tender you like them. Keep warm.

In a blender or food processor, mix horseradish and cottage cheese. Place in a serving bowl. In a kettle, bring water to a boil. Cook watercress for 5 minutes. Drain. In a blender or food processor, puree watercress and cottage cheese. Pour in a serving bowl.

Poached Plums and Peaches, with Fresh Blueberries and Strawberries

•

1 cup water
¾ cup sugar
4 to 6 small plums
3 to 4 peaches
1 tablespoon vanilla extract
1 cup fresh blueberries
1 pint fresh strawberries
    Few mint leaves (optional)

In a kettle, bring 1 cup water and ½ cup sugar to a boil. Reduce heat and cook for 10 minutes. Add plums and peaches, and poach for 5 minutes. Add vanilla and let cool, then refrigerate for at least 1 hour.

With a slotted spoon, remove plums and peaches from syrup and arrange on a serving platter. Sprinkle on the blueberries and half the strawberries. Puree the remaining strawberries in a blender or food processor, with the remaining ¼ cup sugar. Pour over fruit, garnish with mint leaves. Serve.

	Calories	Cholesterol (mg)	Total Fat (g)	Saturated Fat (g)	Sodium (mg)
Mosaic of Vegetables with a Red Pepper and Tomato Coulis	337	—	6.5	0.9	327
Chicken in a Salt Crust	275	101.0	15.6	4.2	94
Steamed Carrots, New Potatoes, and Leeks	145	—	—	—	20
Horseradish Sauce	35	0.6	0.2	0.1	58
Watercress Sauce	14	0.6	0.2	0.1	58
Poached Plums and Peaches, with Fresh Blueberries and Strawberries	242	—	—	—	—
TOTAL	1,048	102	22.5	5.3	557
% of Total Calories			19	5	

* *Note:* Quantities given indicate nutritional value per serving.

Warm Terrine of Sole, Asparagus, and Scallions

Endive and Beet Salad

Peach Tart

Warm Terrine of Sole, Asparagus, and Scallions

•

*W*hile the term *terrine* may be associated most often with hors d'oeuvres, this delicacy is a substantial main course. It is served with a mushroom and white wine sauce.

For the terrine

¼ cup dry white wine

1 tablespoon fresh tarragon, or 1 teaspoon dried

1 tablespoon minced shallots

3 (¼-pound) filets of sole or flounder

4 egg whites

1¼ cups skim milk

16 asparagus, peeled, trimmed, and steamed 5 minutes

8 scallions, trimmed but left whole

In a mixing bowl, combine wine, tarragon, and shallots. Place fish in this marinade, cover, and refrigerate for approximately 2 hours. (If you like, you can plan ahead and let fish marinate overnight.)

Preheat the oven to 400°F. Remove fish from marinade and reserve marinade. In a food processor or blender, puree two-thirds of the fish for a minute or so. Pour in egg whites and puree for another 2 minutes. Add milk and puree for an additional minute. Set aside.

Cut the remaining fish into ½-inch strips. Lightly oil an oblong baking dish. Pour in half the fish puree. Steam asparagus for 5 minutes, then place asparagus lengthwise on top of puree, add scallions and fish strips, then cover with remaining puree. Seal pan with foil, then prick holes in foil with a fork or knife tip to let steam escape. Place dish in a roasting pan filled with 1 inch of hot water. Bake for 15 minutes.

To unmold terrine, run a knife around the edges. Pour excess liquid into a cup and reserve. Put a serving platter over the baking dish, turn terrine upside down, and unmold.

While the fish is baking, prepare the sauce.

For the sauce

1 tablespoon olive oil

2 shallots, minced

4 button mushrooms, sliced

½ cup finely chopped fresh parsley

½ cup fresh tarragon leaves, or 2 tablespoons dried

2 tablespoons 1% cottage cheese

3 tablespoons nonfat dry milk powder

In a saucepan, heat the oil and sauté the shallots for 3 to 4 minutes, or until golden brown. Add the mushrooms, parsley, and tarragon, then simmer for 5 minutes over low heat. Add the reserved marinade, fish liquid, cottage cheese, and powdered milk. When terrine has finished baking, pour fish liquid off and into sauce mixture. Pour into a blender and liquefy, then return to saucepan and heat for 1 minute.

Note: If desired, decorate top of terrine with fresh parsley or tarragon, or both.

Endive and Beet Salad

◆

4 Belgian endive, leaves separated

2 beets, cooked, peeled, and sliced, or 1 (8-ounce) can sliced beets

½ cup finely chopped fresh parsley

Sherry Vinaigrette (page xviii)

On each salad plate, form a fan using the endive leaves. Place sliced beets at the base, then sprinkle on the parsley. Pour vinaigrette over and serve.

Peach Tart

◆

For the crust

½ pound polyunsaturated margarine

¼ cup soy milk

3 cups unbleached all-purpose flour

1 teaspoon almond extract

For the filling

½ cup bread crumbs or crumbled macaroons

6 ripe peaches, peeled, pits removed, and sliced

1 tablespoon sugar

1 teaspoon vanilla extract

2 teaspoons almond extract or Amaretto

Juice of ½ lemon

1 tablespoon polyunsaturated margarine

By hand or with a food processor, combine margarine, milk, flour, and 1 teaspoon almond extract to form a smooth dough. Refrigerate for 30 minutes.

Preheat the oven to 375°F. Line a pie pan with the dough, prick with a fork, and bake for 15 minutes. Let cool.

Line pie crust with crumbs. Lay in the peach slices in a spiral, starting from the edge and working your way to the center. Sprinkle the sugar, vanilla, almond extract, and lemon over the peaches, then dot with margarine. Bake for 30 minutes. Serve either warm or cold. (*Serves 8.*)

	Calories	Cholesterol (mg)	Total Fat (g)	Saturated Fat (g)	Sodium (mg)
Warm Terrine of Sole, Asparagus, and Scallions	216	43	1.1	—	138
Endive and Beet Salad	142	—	13.6	1.8	135
Peach Tart	432	—	25.4	4.5	367
TOTAL	790	43	40.1	6.3	640
% of Total Calories			46	7	

* *Note:* Quantities given indicate nutritional value per serving.

Menu

11

**Marinated Eggplant with Tofu, and
Dried Tomatoes**

Grilled Salmon with Leek Angel Hair

Seasonal Green Salad

Gratin of Strawberries

Marinated Eggplant with Tofu and Dried Tomatoes

*B*oth eggplant and tofu are bright stars in the no-cholesterol constellation. Soybeans and their derivatives have demonstrated an ability to reduce LDL (bad) cholesterol dramatically while also raising HDL (good) cholesterol. Further, eggplant is purported to help protect arteries from cholesterol damage. But the many positive effects of this recipe, however, do not detract one iota from its gourmet appeal. I offer it as a first course, but it is substantial enough—with the tofu standing in for the traditional mozzarella—to be a perfect luncheon main course.

    4 tablespoons olive oil
    1 eggplant, peeled and thinly sliced
 ½ cup balsamic vinegar,
      approximately
    1 small onion, minced
    8 ounces Tofu, in 1-inch cubes

 ½ teaspoon dried thyme
 ½ teaspoon dried oregano
    Few leaves of fresh basil
 ½ cup finely chopped dried tomatoes
    3 scallions, finely chopped
 ½ cup finely chopped fresh parsley
    1 bunch arugula, shredded
    1 red bell pepper, minced

In a skillet, heat 2 tablespoons of the oil and brown the eggplant on both sides. Place in a bowl and cover with balsamic vinegar.

In the same skillet, heat the remaining oil and sauté the onion until light brown. Stir in the tofu and cook over medium heat for 15 minutes, then add the thyme, oregano, and basil.

On a serving platter, place eggplant in the center, then top with the onion-and-tofu mixture and the dried tomatoes. Sprinkle scallions and parsley on top, and surround platter with arugula, on top of which sprinkle the red pepper. Serve.

Grilled Salmon with Leek Angel Hair

*S*almon is a substantial fish, and although even good fish markets recommend about one half-pound of filet per person, I have found that to be a touch too much. If, however, you find my portions on the slim side, adjust for your own appetite. This method of grilling the salmon skin side down only is called in France: "unilateral."

For the salmon

1½ *pounds salmon filet, skin on*
1 *tablespoon olive oil*
Juice of ½ lemon

For the leeks

2 *cups peanut or vegetable oil, for deep-frying*
2 *leeks, washed, trimmed, and cut in spaghetti-thin strips*
Coarse salt

Brush the skin side of the filet evenly with the oil. Sprinkle lemon juice on the other side. Prepare grill. When ready, grill the fish on the skin side for roughly 10 minutes, until whitened. The unilateral method cooks the fish al dente; if you prefer your fish thoroughly cooked, grill for an extra few minutes.

While salmon is cooking, heat the oil in a saucepan. Pat the leeks dry. When oil is hot, deep-fry leeks for 10 minutes. When crisp, remove with a slotted spoon and drain well on absorbent paper.

The fish and leeks should be ready at about the same time. Transfer fish to a serving platter and sprinkle lightly with coarse salt. Crown with leeks.

Seasonal Green Salad

Assorted greens (mâche, arugula, dandelion, watercress)
Vinaigrette of your choice (page xviii)

Wash and dry greens. Tear into bite-size pieces and dress with vinaigrette.

Gratin of Strawberries

*S*trawberries, like most fruit, have many healing properties. In addition to being one of nature's wonders, they have an almost irresistible taste and fragrance. French gastronomy offers many gratinée desserts featuring fruit; the only problem is that the ingredients are usually cream and eggs, both high on the anti-cholesterol most-wanted list. This gratin uses egg whites and skim milk, but it has lost little or none of its original succulent French charm.

2 *teaspoons almond extract*
½ *cup unseasoned breadcrumbs*
1 *tablespoon skim milk*
1 *tablespoon powdered skim milk*
3 *egg whites, whipped until stiff*
1 *quart strawberries, hulled and sliced*

Preheat the broiler. Combine the almond extract, breadcrumbs, and two milks. Then fold into egg whites. In a lightly oiled broiler-proof dish (8 to 10 inches round), form a layer of strawberries. Top with egg white mixture. Place under broiler for a few minutes until the gratin is amber. Serve at once.

Note: Individual broilers vary widely; watch gratin to prevent burning.

	Calories	Cholesterol (mg)	Total Fat (g)	Saturated Fat (g)	Sodium (mg)
Marinated Eggplant with Tofu and Dried Tomatoes	218	—	15.9	2.0	12
Grilled Salmon with Leek Angel Hair	405	94	24.5	3.9	274
Seasonal Green Salad	125	—	13.5	1.8	100
Gratin of Strawberries	118	0.5	0.6	0.2	144
TOTAL	866	94.5	54.5	7.9	530
% of Total Calories			57	8	

* *Note:* Quantities given indicate nutritional value per serving.

Cèpes à la Provençale

Cornish Hens with Baked Garlic

Braised Fennel

Caramelized Apples on Thin Pastry

Cèpes à la Provençale

*C*èpes are large, wide wild mushrooms, ranging in color from beige to purple. In Europe, when cèpes make their autumn appearance it is a gastronomic event, since they are relatively rare and short-lived. While in America you will not find them at your local supermarket, more and more specialty and gourmet grocers are now carrying them. For this recipe, it is imperative that you use fresh cèpes. The Italian equivalent is porcini, and this distinguished first-cousin of the cèpe can be substituted.

1 tablespoon virgin olive oil
4 medium or 2 large cèpes, wiped clean and cut in 1-inch pieces
1 cup finely chopped fresh parsley
3 garlic cloves, minced
   Fresh pepper and salt to taste

In a medium no-stick skillet, heat the oil over medium heat, then sauté the cèpes for 8 minutes. Add the parsley and garlic. Continue cooking for 2 more minutes. Season to taste and serve.

Cornish Hens with Baked Garlic

*I*f you think that this menu is garlic laden, bear in mind that when cooked, the garlic loses its pungency and becomes mellow and sweet.

3 tablespoons olive oil, plus some for sprinkling over hens
4 Cornish hens or squab, skins removed
1 tablespoon paprika
1 tablespoon ground cumin
1 tablespoon dry mustard
   Salt
1 head garlic, loose skins removed and cloves separated but not peeled

Preheat the oven to 350°F. In a kettle, heat 2 tablespoons oil, then brown the hens on all sides over medium heat. Remove from kettle and place in an ovenproof dish.

In a small bowl, mix the paprika, cumin, mustard, and touch of salt. Coat the hens with the spice mixture, then trickle a few drops of oil over them. Roast hens for 20 minutes.

Add garlic to pan and remaining oil. Continue baking for another 15 minutes, occasionally turning cloves so they roast evenly. Serve the hens with the baked garlic cloves on top.

Braised Fennel
•

4 *fennel bulbs, trimmed and cut crosswise*
1–2 *tablespoons olive oil*
Fresh pepper and salt to taste

In a kettle, bring water to a boil. Immerse the fennel and cook for 10 minutes, then drain.

Heat the oil over low heat and brown fennel on all sides. Season to taste with pepper and salt. Serve with the game hens.

Caramelized Apples on Thin Pastry
•

½ *cup unbleached all-purpose flour*
⅓ *cup oat flour*
1 *tablespoon ice water*
10 *tablespoons polyunsaturated margarine*

3 *large apples, peeled, cored, and sliced*
½ *cup sugar*

Using a food processor or by hand, combine the flours and ice water with 4 tablespoons of the margarine. Make a stiff dough, then wrap and refrigerate for 30 minutes.

Unwrap dough, and roll out onto a floured board. Spread 4 tablespoons margarine over dough. Fold as you would a letter, in 3 parts, then refrigerate for another 30 minutes. Roll, fold, and refrigerate twice more.

Preheat the oven to 375°F. Remove dough from refrigerator, roll out, and fit dough into a 10-inch pie pan. With a fork, prick some holes and bake crust for 20 minutes. Place apples in a spiral pattern on the crust. Dot with remaining margarine and bake for an additional 20 minutes. Let cool.

In a saucepan, melt and cook the sugar over medium heat, until it turns amber. *Immediately* (careful, sugar burns in seconds at that crucial point) pour warm sugar over the tart. It will caramelize as it cools. (*Serves 8.*)

	Calories	Cholesterol (mg)	Total Fat (g)	Saturated Fat (g)	Sodium (mg)
Cèpes á la Provençale	58	—	3.4	0.5	170
Cornish Hens with Baked Garlic	516	204	25.0	5.5	225
Braised Fennel	70	—	7.0	1.0	170
Caramelized Apples on Thin Pastry	297	—	14.5	2.5	192
TOTAL	941	204	49.9	9.5	757
% of Total Calories			48	9	

* *Note:* Quantities given indicate nutritional value per serving.

Oyster Ravioli in Parsley Broth

Quenelles of Carrot on a Bed of Cèpes

Warm Pears Gâteau with Blueberry Coulis

Oyster Ravioli in Parsley Broth

*T*his ravioli is made with a much lighter dough than the traditional Italian dish. It is more like Chinese dumplings, which consist primarily of flour and water. Since oysters vary greatly in size, you may need to adjust the recipe and use large oysters cut in half.

For the dough

1½ *cups unbleached all-purpose flour*
½ *cup hot water*
1 *tablespoon olive oil*

For the broth

1 *carrot, peeled and julienned*
1 *celery stalk, peeled and diced*
1 *small leek, trimmed and julienned*
1 *large bunch parsley, finely chopped*
  Juice of 1 lemon
½ *cup dry white wine*
½ *teaspoon dried thyme*
½ *teaspoon dried tarragon*
  Fresh pepper and salt to taste

For the filling

16 *small oysters, shucked, with their liquor, or 8 large, halved*
½ *cup finely chopped fresh parsley*
4 *scallions, finely chopped*

Using a food processor or by hand, combine dough ingredients to form a smooth dough. Wrap and refrigerate for 15 minutes. (You can leave it overnight, if preparing in advance.)

In a kettle, cook the carrot, celery, parsley, and leek in 2 quarts of water, covered, over medium heat for 10 minutes. Add the lemon juice, white wine, and seasonings to kettle. Keep hot.

Make the ravioli filling. Immerse the oysters for 5 seconds (in broth, in and out, using a slotted spoon). Set aside. Roll out ravioli dough as thin as possible on a floured surface. With a knife, divide into 16 rectangles, roughly 2 by 4 inches each. On each rectangle, sprinkle a bit of parsley and scallions. Place 1 oyster in the center of each rectangle. Fold over both flaps and seal by pinching dough together with your fingers. (To give a more professional look, use a fork to pinch edges together.) Gently immerse raviolis in boiling broth. Reduce heat to simmer, and cook for 5 minutes. Serve piping hot.

Quenelles of Carrot on a Bed of Cèpes

For the quenelles

5 *carrots, peeled and sliced*
2 *tablespoons olive oil*
1½ *cups bread cubes (from day-old bread)*
6 *tablespoons all-purpose flour*
2 *egg whites*
1 *onion, minced*
½ *cup wheat bran*
1 *cup finely chopped fresh parsley*
⅓ *cup 1% cottage cheese*
1 *teaspoon freshly grated nutmeg*
Fresh pepper and salt to tate

For the cèpes

½ *cup olive oil*
2 *shallots, minced*
3 *large cèpes, wiped clean, trimmed, and sliced*
1 *cup finely chopped fresh parsley*
Fresh pepper and salt to taste

In a kettle, bring 2 cups water to a boil. Add carrots and cook for 10 minutes. Drain. In a skillet, heat the oil and fry the bread cubes until light brown. Using a food processor, puree the carrots, flour, egg whites, onion, wheat bran, parsley, cottage cheese, nutmeg, pepper, and salt. Add the bread cubes and mix. Refrigerate for 1 hour, covered.

With a knife or spoon, divide carrot mixture in half. Using your hands, form 2 long, sausagelike rolls.

In a large kettle, bring 1 quart water to a boil, then carefully drop carrot "sausages" into the water, using 2 slotted spoons or a spatula for support. Reduce the heat and simmer for 15 minutes. Again using slotted spoons, transfer to absorbent paper and cut "sausages" into half-inch slices while still hot. Place slices in an ovenproof dish, cover, and keep warm in the oven.

Cèpes are large (sometimes very large) mushrooms, the caps of which are often 5 to 8 inches wide, available in France only for a brief period in the fall. In Italy the equivalent is known as porcini. Cèpes are now quite widely available in the United States, including some supermarkets, as are porcini and the Japanese shiitake variety. For this recipe, 3 large cèpes or porcini will suffice, or 1 pound shiitake.

In a skillet, heat olive oil and sauté shallots until golden. Add the cèpes, stir, and cook for 8 minutes. Add the parsley, then transfer to a serving plate. Top cèpes with quenelles. Season with pepper and salt and serve.

Note: If fresh cèpes or porcini are unavailable, substitute 1 pound fresh button mushrooms and ½ cup reconstituted porcini, or use fresh shiitakes.

Warm Pears Gâteau with Blueberry Coulis

•

For the gâteau

6 *egg whites*

1 *egg yolk beaten with 2 tablespoons nonfat dry milk*

1½ *cups unbleached all-purpose flour*

1 *cup skim milk, warmed*

2 *tablespoons rum*

1 *tablespoon almond extract*

1 *tablespoon peanut oil*

3 *pears, peeled, cored, and sliced*

½ *cup wheat germ mixed with ½ cup bran cereal*

½ *cup slivered almonds*

⅔ *tablespoon polyunsaturated margarine, in pieces*

For the coulis

1 *pint ripe blueberries*

¼ *cup sugar*

Preheat the oven to 375°F. In a mixing bowl, combine the egg whites, yolk, flour, milk, rum, extract, and oil. Lightly oil an 8- or 10-inch round baking dish. Pour batter in bowl, then lay pear slices over. Sprinkle with the wheat-germ mixture and almonds. Dot with margarine and bake for 30 to 35 minutes.

In a blender or food processor, puree the blueberries and sugar, then transfer to a small pitcher. When the gâteau is ready, serve on dessert plates and cover with coulis. Serve warm. (*Serves 8.*)

	Calories	Cholesterol (mg)	Total Fat (g)	Saturated Fat (g)	Sodium (mg)
Oyster Ravioli in Parsley Broth	380	—	3.4	0.5	290
Quenelles of Carrot on a Bed of Cèpes	529	10	33.8	4.5	280
Warm Pear Gâteau with Blueberry Coulis	314	34	9.6	1.5	120
TOTAL	1,223	44	46.8	6.5	690
% of Total Calories			34	5	

* *Note:* Quantities given indicate nutritional value per serving.

The (Almost) No Cholesterol Gourmet Cookbook

Menu

14

Vegetable Consommé

Roast Pheasant with Chestnuts
on a Bed of Choucroute

Endive Compote

Cold Apricot Soufflé

*T*his is a gala menu, recommended for New Year's Eve or any other celebratory occasion. If at first glance it appears somewhat richer than most in this book, it has nonetheless been conceived in keeping with our low-cholesterol guidelines. The cabbage, long underestimated for its therapeutic qualities, is a definite plus here, as is the apricot. True, the dark meat of the pheasant is richer than chicken. But to offset that minor sin we start the meal with a light, aromatic consommé, and end it with a light dessert as well. All in all, you can serve and celebrate without a tinge of guilt. Well, perhaps a tinge. . . .

Vegetable Consommé

*

2 *carrots, peeled and julienned*

1 *onion, stuck with 2 whole cloves*

1 *leek, trimmed and cut thin*

1 *celery stalk, peeled and diced*

1 *turnip, peeled and julienned*

   Pinch of dried thyme

   Pinch of dried tarragon

⅓ *cup Sherry*

½ *cup finely chopped fresh parsley*

   Fresh pepper and salt

In a kettle filled with 1 quart of water, put in the vegetables, thyme, and tarragon, and bring to a boil. Reduce heat to medium and cook for 30 minutes. Stir in Sherry. Sprinkle on parsley. Season to taste with salt and pepper. Serve piping hot.

Roast Pheasant with Chestnuts on a Bed of Choucroute

•

For the pheasant

1 pound fresh or canned chestnuts
1 tablespoon olive oil, plus
    additional for coating pheasant
1 onion, minced
¼ pound ground turkey meat
1 teaspoon dried tarragon
½ teaspoon paprika
½ cup finely chopped fresh parsley
1 celery stalk, peeled and diced
¼ cup soy milk
½ cup bread crumbs
1 pheasant, about 3 or 4 pounds
    Fresh pepper and salt

If you opt for fresh chestnuts, make an *x* incision in each with a kitchen knife, then boil for 15 minutes. While the chestnuts are still warm, peel off both husk and inner skin. If using canned chestnuts, drain and rinse well.

Preheat the oven to 400°F. In a skillet, heat the oil and sauté the onion until golden. Add the turkey and cook for 15 minutes over medium heat. Stir in the tarragon, paprika, and parsley. In a mixing bowl, combine celery, soy milk, and bread crumbs with contents of skillet and chestnuts. Mix well, then use to stuff the pheasant. Truss. Pour a few drops of olive oil over the bird and pepper and salt lightly. Place the pheasant in a roasting pan. Put the pheasant in the oven and immediately turn the heat down to 350°F. Roast for 40 minutes. Keep warm while choucroute finishes cooking.

For the choucroute

1 tablespoon olive oil
1 pound sauerkraut, rinsed twice
    under running water and squeezed
    dry
1 cup dry white wine, approximately
1 tablespoon juniper berries
    Fresh pepper and salt to taste

In a saucepan, heat the oil and add the sauerkraut, wine, juniper berries, and seasonings. Cover and cook over low heat for 1 hour. If it seems a little dry, add a bit more white wine.

Endive Compote

•

5 Belgian endive, chopped
2 tablespoons olive oil
    Juice of 1 lemon
½ cup minced fresh parsley
½ teaspoon grated nutmeg
    Fresh pepper and salt to taste

In a kettle, bring 1 quart water to a boil. Cook the endive for 5 minutes, then drain. In a saucepan, heat the oil, add the endive with the lemon juice, half the parsley, and the nutmeg. Cover and cook over low heat for 20 minutes. Season with pepper and salt.

In a blender or food processor, puree the endive and return to saucepan. Five minutes before serving, reheat gently, then sprinkle on remaining parsley.

Spoon choucroute onto a platter to form a thin layer. Place the pheasant on the choucroute and the endive compote on the side.

Cold Apricot Soufflé

•

1 pound plus 6 dried apricots,
  soaked 30 minutes in water and
  drained

¼ cup sugar

1 tablespoon cornstarch, diluted in
  1 tablespoon soy milk

½ cup soy milk

1 tablespoon unflavored gelatin,
  dissolved in juice of 1 lemon

3 egg whites, beaten until stiff

In a food processor or blender, puree the apricots with the sugar. Set aside. In a small saucepan, heat the cornstarch and soy milk over low heat. Bring to a boil, reduce heat to very low, and cook for 2 minutes. Turn off heat and stir in the gelatin. Add apricot puree, continuing to stir. Cool well. Gently fold egg whites into apricot mixture. Pour into a soufflé dish and refrigerate for at least 3 hours (overnight preferred). (*Serves 4.*)

Note: If desired, decorate soufflé with candied apricots. Coat 6 reconstituted and drained apricots with 1 egg white. Then roll in ¼ cup sugar, coating well on both sides. Refrigerate overnight. Use the candied apricots to form a flower. If you have some mint leaves, add to simulate leaves.

	Calories	Cholesterol (mg)	Total Fat (g)	Saturated Fat (g)	Sodium (mg)
Vegetable Consommé	35	—	—	—	250
Roast Pheasant with Chestnuts on a Bed of Choucroute	531	78	11.8	2.4	901
Endive Compote	70	—	6.5	0.9	125
Cold Apricot Soufflé	350	—	0.6	—	40
TOTAL	986	78	18.9	3.3	1,316
% of Total Calories			17	3	

* *Note:* Quantities given indicate nutritional value per serving.

Crown Roast of Lamb

Gâteau of Eggplant

Haricots Verts

Watercress Salad

Floating Peaches and Apples

Crown Roast of Lamb

•

This preparation of lamb, with its paper frills, announces a gala occasion. Ask your butcher to prepare it for you, and remind him to crack the chin bone (this will be important when the roast is carved). In classic French gastronomy the crown roast is most often served with a stuffing, but here the eggplant gâteau elegantly replaces it.

This is a slight digression from the virtually no-cholesterol menus. But to keep things in perspective—at least this is my rationalization—note that there is only one-third the cholesterol in a 3-ounce serving of this lamb as is in a single egg. To further offset the errant main course, serve the dessert, featuring the ever-therapeutic apple.

Note: A crown roast usually comes in a 14- to 16-rib section, to serve 4 people. Remember that the ribs are little more than a mouthful, so 4 rib chops per person equal approximately 1 small loin chop.

1 tablespoon dried thyme
   Freshly ground pepper
1 *crown or rack of lamb, about 1
   pound, dressed*

Preheat the oven to 350°F. Sprinkle the thyme and pepper on the meat. Roast for 45 minutes to 1 hour, depending on whether you prefer your lamb pink or well done. Remove from oven, add paper frills to crown, and serve.

Gâteau of Eggplant

◆

2 tablespoons olive oil

1 onion, minced

1 eggplant, peeled and diced

4 ounces tofu

1 garlic clove, minced

¼ cup bran cereal

¼ cup wheat germ

¼ cup bread crumbs

6 egg whites

Preheat the oven to 350°F. In a skillet, heat the oil and sauté the onion until translucent. Add the eggplant and cook over low heat, adding a little water to keep it from sticking; after roughly 15 minutes, eggplant should be soft. Transfer to a food processor and puree with the remaining ingredients.

Brush an 8-inch baking dish lightly with olive oil, transfer mixture to dish, and bake for 25 minutes, until it rises slightly and turns golden.

Haricots Verts

◆

1 pound extra-thin green beans, trimmed and whole

½ cup finely chopped fresh parsley

2 tablespoons polyunsaturated margarine

Fresh pepper and salt

Steam the beans for 5 minutes, then drain. Toss with the parsley and margarine. Season to taste and serve.

Watercress Salad

◆

1 bunch watercress

Vinaigrette (page xviii)

Wash and trim the watercress, then dress with vinaigrette.

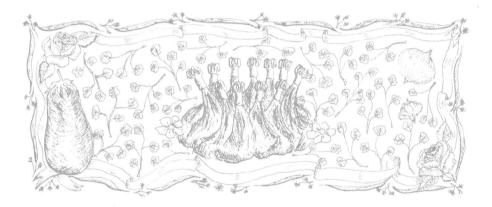

Floating Peaches and Apples

I have never been able to entirely give up the dessert the French call *Les iles flot-tantes*—"Floating Islands." However, it is a cholesterol booby trap, packed as it is with egg yolks and cream. This version has most of its delectable virtues without its defects.

½ cup sugar
½ cup slivered almonds
3 cups vanilla nonfat yogurt
½ cup Sauternes or other sweet white wine
¼ cup Amaretto
2 apples, cored and sliced
2 ripe peaches, peeled, pits removed, and sliced

In a saucepan, melt the sugar, then stir in the almonds over low heat until mixture turns amber. Quickly spread the contents of the pan on a sheet of foil to cool.

In a deep serving dish, combine the yogurt, wine, and Amaretto. Stir in the apples and peaches. Sprinkle top with caramelized almonds, then refrigerate for at least 1 hour. Serve chilled. (*Serves 8.*)

	Calories	Cholesterol (mg)	Total Fat (g)	Saturated Fat (g)	Sodium (mg)
Crown Roast of Lamb	325	70	28.0	5.0	35
Gâteau of Eggplant	169	—	8.5	0.9	75
Haricots Verts	83	—	5.7	1.0	119
Watercress Salad	100	—	10.0	1.4	135
Floating Peaches and Apples	177	—	3.0	—	—
TOTAL	854	70	55.2	8.3	364
% of Total Calories			58	9	

* *Note:* Quantities given indicate nutritional value per serving.

Menu

16

Chilled Cream of Artichoke Soup

Venison à la Jacques Français

Gâteau of Potatoes

Watercress Salad

Fresh Pineapple and Strawberries

Chilled Cream of Artichoke Soup

*I*n recent studies carried out around the world, the artichoke—already recognized as having many therapeutic qualities—has been shown to be effective in lowering blood cholesterol. In addition it is a gourmet delicacy I offer in several forms and varieties in this book.

    5 *large artichokes*
    2 *cups skim milk*
       Juice of ½ lemon
    1 *chicken-flavored bouillon cube*
    2 *cups chicken stock*
    1 *cup finely chopped fresh parsley*

Fresh pepper and salt
1 *tablespoon cornstarch*
½ *cup plain low-fat yogurt*

In a large kettle, bring 3 quarts of water to a boil. Cook the artichokes for 35 to 40 minutes, or until the leaves detach easily. Drain and remove all leaves. (Reserve leaves for a later vinaigrette.) Scrape out the chokes, leaving the hearts. In a food processor, puree the artichoke hearts with the milk, lemon juice, bouillon cube, stock, parsley, pepper, and cornstarch. Return to kettle, bring to a boil, and cook 5 minutes over low heat. Let cool, then stir in yogurt. Salt to taste, and refrigerate several hours before serving.

Venison à la Jacques Français

*J*acques Français is not only one of the world's experts in the realm of stringed instruments but also a fine cook and gourmet. Our musical association goes back many years, but it was not until relatively recently that we became aware of our mutual interest in food. This is one of my favorite recipes from his repertory. Venison is readily available in autumn in most places and can be found at good butchers.

> 4 venison steaks, ½ inch thick
> ⅓ cup olive oil
> 1 onion, minced
> 3 carrots, peeled and julienned
> 3 celery stalks, peeled and julienned
> 1 teaspoon dried thyme
> 1 teaspoon ground bay leaf
> 1 teaspoon freshly ground black pepper
> ½ cup dry white wine
> 2 tablespoons vinegar

Prepare grill. When coals are ready, grill venison 4 to 5 minutes on each side. (If grill is unavailable, broiling is fine.) In a medium saucepan, heat the oil and sauté the onion until translucent. Add the carrots and celery, then stir in the thyme, bay leaf, and ½ teaspoon pepper. Cook for 5 minutes or until vegetables are soft.

In a blender or food processor, puree the mixture, then return to saucepan. Add the wine and vinegar, and remaining pepper. Cook over low heat for 5 minutes.

Place steaks on a serving platter. Pour on vegetable puree and serve.

Gâteau of Potatoes

I first had this dish—which takes the ordinary potato and turns it into something wonderfully festive—at what was then a relatively little-known but highly appreciated Paris bistro called l'Ami Louis. For better or worse, this little restaurant, with its dark-stained walls, narrow tables, and caring waiters, has become so well-known that it's impossible to get a reservation these days. But the l'Ami Louis potato cake lingered in my memory. I have slightly modified the texture, but the flavor is the same.

> ¼ cup olive oil
> 4 medium potatoes, scrubbed and julienned
> ½ cup finely chopped fresh parsley
> 4 garlic cloves, minced.

Heat the oil in a large skillet. With a fork, spread the potatoes evenly, and cook over low to medium heat for about 10 minutes, until the bottom becomes crisp. (To check, lift gently with a fork.) With a spatula, lift the potato cake and flip it over. (If necessary, add a few drops of oil to moisten skillet.) Cook another 10 minutes or so, until second side is crisp and golden.

Turn off heat. With a fork, press the parsley and minced garlic into the potato cake. Place the gâteau on a serving platter and cut into portions as you would a cake.

Watercress Salad

1 bunch watercress, trimmed
Sherry Vinaigrette (page xviii)

Wash watercress thoroughly. Dry well. Pour Sherry vinaigrette, toss and serve.

Fresh Pineapple and Strawberries

1 ripe pineapple
1 pint fresh strawberries, hulled but whole
Few fresh mint leaves

Slice the pineapple lengthwise into quarters. With a knife, cut out pineapple flesh, eliminating core. Cube edible part and replace in shell, interspersed with strawberries. Strew mint leaves on top. Serve.

	Calories	Cholesterol (mg)	Total Fat (g)	Saturated Fat (g)	Sodium (mg)
Chilled Cream of Artichoke Soup	164	—	1.0	—	845
Venison à la Jacques Français	340	60	18.0	1.8	70
Gâteau of Potatoes	245	—	13.5	1.8	—
Watercress Salad	108	—	10.4	1.4	179
Fresh Pineapple and Strawberries	342	—	13.5	1.8	—
TOTAL	1,199	60	56.4	6.8	1,094
% of Total Calories			39	5	

* *Note:* Quantities given indicate nutritional value per serving.

Menu

17

Brandade of Flageolets
with My Toulouse Sausage

Chicory Salad

Peach Cobbler with Caramelized Almonds

Brandade of Flageolets with My Toulouse Sausage

·

*T*his is an adaptation of a French peasant dish that is especially prevalent in the southwest. In its traditional incarnation, the sausage is made with pork and *gras double* (literally, "double fat"—a slice of pork containing mostly fat). Obviously that recipe poses some problems for this book, so I substitute turkey for the pork and tofu for the *gras double*. I also use olive oil instead of lard or butter. While I do not claim that this version matches the substance of the original, from the point of view of taste it is an honorable approximation. Should you not have access to flageolets, (French dried green beans), white kidney beans do fine.

For the brandade

1 *pound flageolets, soaked in water to cover and drained*

¼ *cup olive oil, approximately*

2 *large onions, minced*

1 *teaspoon dried thyme*

1 *teaspoon dried tarragon*

1 *tablespoon dried basil*

1 *teaspoon dried oregano*

½ *teaspooon ground bay leaf*

½ *teaspoon freshly ground black pepper*

1 *carrot, peeled and sliced*

1 *cup finely chopped fresh parsley, plus a little extra*

3 *garlic cloves, minced, plus a little extra*

2 *firm squares tofu, cut in 1-inch cubes*

For the sausage

1 pound ground turkey breast

2 egg whites

*2 slices whole wheat bread, soaked
and squeezed dry*

½ cup chopped fresh parsley

3 garlic cloves, minced

1 teaspoon salt

*4 tablespoons polyunsaturated
margarine*

*½ teaspoon ground black pepper
Few sausage casings*

1 tablespoon olive oil

Both parts of this recipe—the sausage and the brandade—can be prepared ahead of time. To make the brandade, bring 2 quarts of water to a boil in a large pot. Drop in the flageolets, return to a boil, reduce heat, cover, and cook for 45 minutes. Test to see if beans are done (white beans take somewhat longer than flageolets). Drain in a colander and reserve 1 cup of the liquid.

Using the same kettle, heat the oil and sauté the onions until light brown. Add the herbs, pepper, and carrot, then cook for 10 minutes over medium heat, stirring constantly. Add the beans. If the beans appear dry, lubricate with some of the reserved liquid and a bit more oil. Toss in parsley and garlic, then cook an additional 5 minutes.

In a food processor or blender, puree bean mixture, then return it to kettle. Add the tofu, plus a bit more parsley and garlic. Adjust seasoning to taste.

To make the sausage, puree half the turkey, in a food processor or by hand, with all remaining ingredients except the casings and oil. By hand, coarsely chop the remaining turkey, and combine with the pureed ingredients. I always have on hand a store of sausage casings, which I keep packed in salt, in the refrigerator, from my butcher. If you do, make sure you rinse the casings in cold water to rid them of any salt. (Fit the casing end over the faucet and let the cold water run through.) Fit the casing onto a sausage maker and fill with turkey puree. Make a half-dozen sausages, each about 6 to 8 inches long. Tie the sausages tightly at each end.

Prick sausages with a fork. In a skillet, heat olive oil and sauté the sausages gently over low heat until light brown on all sides.

Note: If you can't obtain casings from your butcher, or do not care to use casings, simply shape the sausages with your hands, then roll them in flour and chill for 1 hour. (Manual sausage makers are inexpensive and are available at local kitchen appliance stores; also, many kitchen appliances have a sausage-maker attachment.)

Chicory Salad

In France, the entire head of chicory is yellow and deliciously usable for salads. In America, only the center is tender, so you might need two heads, depending on seasonal produce. I like this salad especially in tandem with the main course, because its crispness complements the soft richness of the brandade.

1 or 2 heads chicory
*Vinaigrette of your choice (page
xviii)*

Wash and dry chicory. Dress with vinaigrette.

Peach Cobbler with Caramelized Almonds

½ cup almonds

⅓ cup granulated sugar

½ cup bran

1 cup whole wheat flour

½ cup brown sugar

½ teaspoon salt

3 egg whites

1 tablespoon evaporated skim milk

½ cup skim milk

4 tablespoons unsalted
polyunsaturated margarine

1 tablespoon Amaretto

1 tablespoon baking soda

3 cups peeled and sliced peaches

In a skillet, toast almonds with sugar over low heat, stirring constantly, until they turn amber. Place caramelized almonds on a sheet of foil and set aside. When cool, break into small pieces.

Preheat the oven to 400°F. In a mixing bowl, mix bran, flour, brown sugar, salt, egg whites, both milks, margarine, Amaretto, and baking soda, to form a sticky dough with your hands. (This can be done in a food processor as well.) Lightly oil a 10-inch baking dish. Cover bottom with a layer of peaches. Sprinkle on the caramelized almonds. With your fingers, cover the peaches and almonds with the dough. Bake for 20 to 25 minutes. Serve warm. (Serves 8.)

Note: If desired, top servings with nonfat vanilla yogurt.

	Calories	Cholesterol (mg)	Total Fat (g)	Saturated Fat (g)	Sodium (mg)
Brandade of Flageolets with My Toulouse Sausage	811	96	43.9	6.4	1,037
Chicory Salad	136	—	10.8	1.4	217
Peach Cobbler with Caramelized Almonds	500	—	10.3	1.0	82
TOTAL	1,447	96	65	7.4	1,336
% of Total Calories			40	5	

* *Note:* Quantities given indicate nutritional value per serving.

Menu

18

The Russian Tea Room Remembered...

Vegetable Borscht with My Sour Cream and Piroshki

Blinis with Caviar

Raspberry, Cherry, and Cranberry Kissel

Long before dining out became one of this country's favorite pastimes, there was a culinary jewel in the heart of Manhattan, "slightly to the left of Carnegie Hall," as the now-famous advertisement describes it: the Russian Tea Room. For the thousands who have dined there, the festively decorated rooms, with their garlands of sparkling gold lights, the red-and-white tablecloths, the waiters dressed like Russian dancers, the consistently good fare conjure up exotic glamour that remains unsurpassed despite the proliferation of other fine restaurants, Russian or otherwise. It was one of the first restaurants I went to when I arrived in America, and in the ensuing years I have sampled virtually every dish offered there; the borscht and blinis, especially, remain irresistible. In this menu I have tried to re-create (as honorably as possible without resorting to butter, eggs, cream, or sour cream) some of these delectable Russian dishes.

Vegetable Borscht with My Sour Cream and Piroshki

There are two kinds of borscht: one made with beef and beef and pork bones; the other made only with vegetables. The meat version is more substantial, richer, and perhaps tastier than its vegetarian cousin, but by adroitly balancing the spicing, I have a vegetable borscht that compares favorably with the meat version.

For the borscht

2 tablespoons olive oil

1 large onion, minced

3 potatoes, peeled and cubed

½ cup chopped fresh dill, or 1
  tablespoon dried

6 beets, peeled and shredded, or 3
  (8-ounce) cans shredded beets

2 carrots, peeled and sliced

3 tomatoes, peeled and cubed

1 celery stalk, peeled and diced
  Juice of 1 lemon

8 cups beef stock

1 garlic clove, minced

1 cup sauerkraut, rinsed, or ½ green
  cabbage, shredded

1 tablespoon sugar

¼ cup red wine vinegar
  Fresh pepper and salt to taste

For my sour cream

1 (8-ounce) container 1% cottage
  cheese

½ cup low-fat yogurt
  Minced fresh dill

In a kettle, heat the oil and sauté the onion
until translucent. Add the potatoes, dill, beets,
carrots, tomatoes, celery, lemon juice, stock,
garlic, sauerkraut or cabbage, sugar, and vinegar. Bring to a boil, reduce heat, and cook,
covered, for 20 minutes.

With a slotted spoon, scoop out about half
the vegetables and, adding 3 to 4 cups of the
soup liquid, puree in a blender or food processor. (By so doing you'll get a smoother, cream-
ier borscht than if you left the vegetables
intact.) Return contents of blender to kettle,
stir. Season to taste with pepper and salt, and
adding a bit more dill, if desired. Keep warm
until ready to serve.

While soup cooks, prepare piroshki. Preheat the oven to 375°F. In a skillet, heat 1 tablespoon of the oil and sauté the onion until
light brown. Add the turkey, dill, salt and pepper. Cook over medium heat for 10 minutes,
then turn off heat and mix in cooked egg
whites.

Use the remaining tablespoon of oil to
lightly brush the filo dough. Place 3 oiled
sheets on top of one another, fold in half, and
place 2 tablespoons of filling in the center.
Fold the narrow ends of the dough over the
meat, then turn and roll the piroshki to close
the "package." Proceed until the dough and
filling are used up. Place on cookie sheet and
bake for 20 minutes.

While piroshki bake, liquefy the cottage
cheese in a blender or food processor, smooth-
ing its curd. Mix yogurt and cottage cheese,
then refrigerate until ready to serve.

For the piroshkis

*P*iroshki, the delicate pastry accompaniment offered with borscht, is generally made with a rich, flaky crust, and its
filling is mainly beef. I use filo dough instead,
along with turkey meat.

2 tablespoons olive oil

1 onion, minced

1 pound ground turkey breast

¼ cup finely chopped fresh dill
  Fresh pepper and salt to taste

2 hard-boiled egg whites, mashed

12 to 14 sheets filo dough

Serve the piping hot borscht with a teaspoon
of my sour cream in the center of each serving
and with piroshki on side. Sprinkle the balance
of the "sour cream" with dill in a serving bowl,
to be passed with the borscht, and also to be
served with the main course, the blinis.

The (Almost) No Cholesterol Gourmet Cookbook

Blinis with Caviar

*T*o my mind, these blinis are as tasty as their classic cousin, yet are far healthier since they are made without eggs, butter, or whole milk.

   1 *teaspoon sugar*
   ¾ *cup skim milk, warmed*
   1 *tablespoon active dry yeast*
   ⅓ *cup unbleached all-purpose flour*
   ½ *cup buckwheat flour*
     Pinch of salt
   2 *egg whites, lightly beaten*
   1 *cup finely chopped fresh dill*
   1 *tablespoon My Sour Cream*
     (page 56)
     Oil for cooking
   4 *tablespoons polyunsaturated margarine, melted*
   1 *2-ounce jar red caviar*

In a mixing bowl, dissolve the sugar in ¼ cup skim milk. Add the yeast, then wait for a few minutes until mixture forms a pastelike consistency. Add the flours, salt, and remaining milk. Cover and let rise for at least 2 hours.

Preheat the oven to 200°F. Add the beaten egg whites to the batter, along with 1 tablespoon dill and the sour cream.

Lubricate a skillet with a little oil and heat. Add a ladleful of batter and cook as you would an American pancake. When blinis are cooked, place in a covered dish and keep warm in the oven. Meanwhile, melt the margarine in a saucepan.

Place 2 warm blinis on each plate, pour on a little of the melted margarine, add a tablespoon or so of sour cream, top with a dollop of caviar, and sprinkle with remaining dill.

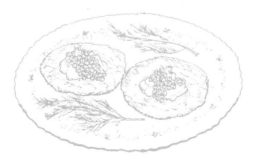

Raspberry, Cherry, and Cranberry Kissel

I love to conclude my Russian Tea Room meals with a kissel, which is simply pureed fruit. This red-hued variety combines the delicate fragrance of raspberries with the sweetness of cherries and the tartness of cranberries. It's best made a day ahead.

3 teaspoons cornstarch
1 pint fresh raspberries
3 cups water
2¼ cups sugar
1 pint fresh cranberries
1 pint fresh cherries, pitted, or 1 (8-ounce) can black cherries

Dissolve 1 teaspoon cornstarch in a few drops of water. Place raspberries in a saucepan with 1 cup water and ¾ cup sugar. Bring to a boil, then stir in cornstarch, reduce heat, and cook for 3 to 4 minutes. Turn off heat and set aside. Proceed in the same manner with the cranberries, and then the cherries, but cook for 10 minutes. Cook the cherries for 3 to 4 minutes.

In a blender or food processor, puree each fruit separately until you have 3 smooth purees. Pour the cranberries into a dessert bowl, and refrigerate for 1 hour. Remove and pour in the cherry puree; again let cool, then remove and pour in raspberry puree. Return dish to refrigerator, to chill for at least 4 hours.

	Calories	Cholesterol (mg)	Total Fat (g)	Saturated Fat (g)	Sodium (mg)
Vegetable Borscht with My Sour Cream and Piroshki	928	96	34.1	6.8	2,110
Blinis with Caviar	275	83	11.9	2.1	303
Raspberry, Cherry and Cranberry Kissel	495	—	—	—	—
TOTAL	1,698	179	46.0	8.9	2,413
% of Total Calories			24	5	

* *Note:* Quantities given indicate nutritional value per serving.

Terrine of Tomato, Black Olives, and Eggplant,
Served with Eggplant Caviar and Tomato Coulis

Steamed Bass with Warm Vinaigrette

New Potatoes with Parsley

Blueberry, Pink Grapefruit, and Campari Sorbet

Terrine of Tomato, Black Olives, and Eggplant, Served with Eggplant Caviar and Tomato Coulis

*T*his is an especially engaging appetizer from both gourmet and health viewpoints, since it combines three vegetables known for their therapeutic value. I also serve this frequently, especially in summer, as a luncheon main course.

2 *large eggplants, peeled and thinly sliced lengthwise*

¼ *cup olive oil, approximately*

4 *large tomatoes, peeled*

1 *cup tomato juice*

1 *(6-ounce) can tomato paste*
  Fresh pepper and salt to taste

2 *(1-ounce) packages unflavored gelatin, softened in 2 tablespoons water*

1 *cup black olives, sliced and pitted*
  Fresh parsley sprigs
  Eggplant Caviar (recipe follows)
  Tomato Coulis (recipe follows)

Preheat oven to 375°F. Place eggplant slices on a baking sheet and brush lightly with olive oil on both sides. Bake for about 20 minutes or until tender.

With a serrated knife, carefully carve off the *outer part only* of the tomatoes, much as you would remove the peel of an orange. Remove any seeds, and gently flatten the tomato "slices."

In a small saucepan, heat the tomato juice, tomato paste, salt and pepper, and softened gelatin. Set aside. Line a 9 × 5-inch loaf pan with waxed paper, making sure that at least 3 inches of paper overhang on all sides. Form a layer with the eggplant slices, making sure they overhang the mold as well. Make a second layer with tomato slices. Pour on 2 tablespoons of the gelatin mixture, then spread a layer of black olives. Add another layer of tomatoes, and top with another layer of eggplant slices. Pour on remaining gelatin mixture. Fold over the eggplant to cover, and then fold over waxed paper on top. Weigh down top with one or more cans, and refrigerate for at least 2 hours (overnight is preferable).

To unmold, place a serving dish over the pan and invert. Gently peel off waxed paper, then decorate loaf with parsley. Slice terrine with a serrated knife, and serve with 1 tablespoon each Eggplant Caviar and Tomato Coulis.

Eggplant Caviar

◆

1 medium eggplant, unpeeled
1 small onion, minced
   Juice of 1 lemon
½ cup finely chopped fresh parsley
½ cup finely chopped fresh coriander (cilantro), optional
⅓ cup olive oil
½ teaspoon red pepper flakes
   Fresh pepper and salt to taste

Place the eggplant over flame of stove (or bake in oven) and char on all sides. Peel off charred skin. (*Note:* to speed the process, rather than wait for eggplant to cool, peel it under cold running water, then pat dry on absorbent paper.) In a blender of food processor, puree eggplant with all remaining ingredients. Transfer to a serving bowl.

Tomato Coulis

◆

2 tablespoons olive oil
1 small onion, minced
3 large tomatoes, peeled and diced
1 tablespoon balsamic vinegar
   Fresh pepper and salt

In a medium skillet, heat the olive oil and sauté the onion until golden. Add the tomato and cook over medium heat for about 10 minutes. Stir in vinegar and pepper and salt to taste. Transfer to a serving bowl.

Steamed Bass with Warm Vinaigrette

◆

2 to 4 sea bass filets, about 2 pounds
1 lemon, sliced
1 sprig fresh tarragon
   Fresh pepper and salt to taste
1½ tablespoons sherry vinegar
1 tablespoon minced shallots
½ cup finely chopped fresh parsley
1 tablespoon olive oil

Preheat the oven to 375°F. Wrap filets in foil, with lemon slices, tarragon, and pepper. Bake for 15 minutes.

Make the vinaigrette in a separate saucepan. Heat the vinegar and add shallots; cook for 3 minutes. Add the parsley, olive oil, and salt and pepper.

When fish is cooked, transfer to a serving platter, pour half the hot vinaigrette over the fish, reserving the remaining vinaigrette to pass at the table.

New Potatoes with Parsley

◆

12 small potatoes
½ cup finely chopped fresh parsley

Cook potatoes in a little water until tender, about 10 minutes. Drain and return to pan. Sprinkle with parsley and cover. Keep warm until ready to serve.

Blueberry, Pink Grapefruit, and Campari Sorbet

.

¾ *cup sugar*

½ *cup water*

1 *cup fresh blueberries*

2 *cups pink grapefruit sections, pulp only*

Juice of 1 lemon

⅓ *cup Campari*

2 *egg whites, beaten until stiff*

In a small saucepan, cook sugar and water over medium heat until syrupy. Cool, then set aside. In a food processor or blender, puree blueberries, grapefruit, lemon juice, and Campari.

Place a bowl with the beaten egg whites over a kettle of simmering hot water. Cook the egg whites, stirring slightly, for 15 minutes, until it is a firm, meringuelike consistency, or Italian meringue. (It is not as hard as the meringues one eats, but it nevertheless holds together.) Combine pureed fruit with sugar syrup and place in freezer for 30 minutes. Place the meringue in the freezer, also for 30 minutes. Remove both and fold together contents of both bowls to form a sorbet. Return to freezer for at least 2 hours. Serve.

	Calories	Cholesterol (mg)	Total Fat (g)	Saturated Fat (g)	Sodium (mg)
Terrine of Tomato, Black Olives, and Eggplant, Served with Eggplant Caviar and Tomato Coulis	743	—	47.1	5.1	903
Steamed Bass with Warm Vinaigrette	360	65	18.3	2.3	190
New Potatoes with Parsley	120	—	0.3	—	24
Blueberry, Pink Grapefruit and Campari Sorbet	185	—	—	—	25
TOTAL	1,408	65	65.7	7.4	1,142
% of Total Calories			42	5	

* *Note:* Quantities given indicate nutritional value per serving.

Menu

20

Oyster Napoleons with Truffle Sauce

Roast Quail in Baked Potato Shells

Timbale of Broccoli

Crown of Assorted Fresh Fruit
with Raspberry Coulis

This is another gala menu that I recommend for an especially festive occasion. But despite the seeming richness of the menu, it is, as you will note from the calorie and cholesterol count at the end, dietetically very reasonable. You can indulge without guilt—and without, if you like, revealing that the menu is as safe as it is savory.

Oyster Napoleons with Truffle Sauce

For the Napoleon

4 tablespoons polyunsaturated
  margarine
1 tablespoon finely minced shallots
2 tablespoons cornstarch
2 cups skim milk

Fresh pepper and salt to taste
½ cup finely chopped fresh parsely
  Juice of ½ lemon
10 button mushrooms, sliced
24 oysters, shucked, with liquor
  reserved
2 tablespoons brandy
  Pastry, see Crust (page 33)

For the sauce

1 tablespoon polyunsaturated
  margarine
1 large unpeeled canned truffle, with
  juice, chopped very fine
1 tablespoon sherry or Madeira
  Fresh pepper to taste

In a large saucepan, melt half the margarine and sauté the shallots until golden brown. Stir in the cornstarch, and gradually add the milk, until the mixture thickens. Pour into a blender and liquefy, then return to saucepan. Add pepper and parsley. Pour lemon juice over mushrooms, and add them to saucepan. Cook over low heat for 5 minutes. Add oysters and their liquor, then turn off heat. Stir in brandy. Season to taste.

Preheat the oven to 400°F. Roll out pastry into a rectangle roughly 8 × 20 inches. Divide into 8 or 10 even rectangles. Prick with a fork, and bake for 10 minutes, then lower oven to 375°F. and bake for another 10 minutes. The pastry is done when the rectangles have puffed high and are golden, showing layers of dough.

Using a serrated knife, cut the puff pastry horizontally into 2 or even 3 layers. With a slotted spoon, spread the oyster filling on each layer of puff pastry, topping last layer with a cover of puff pastry, to form "Napoleons." Place on a cookie sheet and keep warm in a 200°F. oven while you prepare sauce.

In a saucepan, melt margarine, then stir in truffle and juice. Cook over low heat for 2 minutes, turn off heat, and stir in wine. Season with pepper.

When ready to serve, transfer "Napoleons" to individual plates and spoon a little of the sauce over each.

Roast Quail in Baked Potato Shells

•

*B*ecause quail are small, you might consider increasing recipe to serve two per person. But since the appetizer is substantial, one quail each should suffice.

> 4 *baking potatoes*
> 3 *tablespoons olive oil*
> 4 *quail, skin removed*
> 1 *tablespoon ground cumin*
> 1 *tablespoon dry mustard*
>   *Fresh pepper and salt to taste*
> 1 *tablespoon polyunsaturated*
>   *margarine*
> ½ *cup finely chopped fresh parsley*

Preheat the oven to 375°F., then bake potatoes for 1 hour. In a large skillet, heat the oil, reduce heat to medium, and pan-roast quail for 15 minutes, turning once when first side is brown. Mix cumin and mustard, then rub mixture over browned quail.

Cut tops off the potatoes and scoop out a hollow in which to place each quail. In a baking dish, put the quail in their potato skins, add a dot of margarine to each, and sprinkle with parsley, salt, and pepper. Place dish in oven and bake for another 10 to 15 minutes.

Timbale of Broccoli

•

½ head broccoli, chopped
½ teaspoon grated nutmeg
2 tablespoons 1% cottage cheese
  Fresh pepper and salt to taste
2 egg whites, beaten until stiff

Preheat the oven to 375°F. Bring 1 cup of water to a boil in a kettle, cook broccoli at a simmer for 5 minutes. Drain.

In a blender or food processor, puree broccoli with nutmeg, cottage cheese, pepper, and salt. Fold in egg white.

Lightly oil 4 small (4-inch) ovenproof dishes. Pour broccoli mixture into dishes and bake for 20 minutes.

Crown of Assorted Fruit with Raspberry Coulis

•

For the fruit

1 cup fresh raspberries
1 large seedless orange, peeled and sliced
1 pear, peeled, cored, and sliced
1 kiwifruit, peeled and sliced

For the coulis

1 pint fresh raspberries
½ cup sugar

Arrange fruit in a crown on a serving platter. Chill.

In a blender, puree raspberries and sugar. Pour in a serving bowl. Serve with chilled fruit.

	Calories	Cholesterol (mg)	Total Fat (g)	Saturated Fat (g)	Sodium (mg)
Oyster Napoleons with Truffle Sauce	431	54	15.8	9.6	734
Roast Quail in Baked Potato Shells	417	120	14.5	2.4	238
Timbale of Broccoli	31	—	—	—	214
Crown of Assorted Fresh Fruit with Raspberry Coulis	73	—	0.4	—	1
TOTAL	952	174	30.7	12.0	1,187
% of Total Calories			29	11	

* *Note:* Quantities given indicate nutritional value per serving.

The (Almost) No Cholesterol Gourmet Cookbook

Menu

21

A Safe and Light Pâté
of Mushrooms and Chicken

Endive Tart

Mâche and Beet Salad with Walnuts

Cantaloupe Sorbet

A Safe and Light Pâté
of Mushrooms and Chicken

*I*t's all well and good, in the name of medical *sagesse*, to cook and enjoy vegetable and fish pâtés in place of sinful meat pâtés. But there are times when I feel the urge to rebel, and cook a meat pâté that stands the scrutiny of tough cholesterol inspectors. This recipe contains no rich meat, no cream, no eggs (not even whites), no butter, and no pork fat. What, you might wonder, does it contain and still merit the term "pâté"? Read on. (This pâté serves eight, so you'll have some left over for sandwiches the next day.)

1 *onion, quartered*
1 *carrot, peeled*
1 *celery stalk, peeled and chopped*
½ *pound polyunsaturated margarine*
4 *to 5 whole chicken breasts, skin removed, cut into 1-inch pieces*
½ *teaspoon paprika*
½ *teaspoon grated nutmeg*
1 *tablespoon dried tarragon*
½ *teaspoon dried thyme*
  Fresh pepper and salt to taste
½ *pound button mushrooms, sliced*
¼ *cup brandy*
2 *tablespoons unflavored gelatin*
¼ *cup dry white wine*
  Sprigs of parsley, for garnish

In a food processor, chop the onion and set aside. Then chop the carrot and celery together (or julienne by hand). In a large skillet, melt half the margarine, then sauté the onion until golden. Add the carrot and celery, and cook for another 5 minutes over medium heat. Add chicken pieces, then season with paprika, nutmeg, tarragon, thyme, and pepper and salt. Continue cooking over low heat, covered, for 15 to 20 minutes. Transfer to a food processor, reserving 1 cup of chicken pieces.

In the same skillet, melt remaining margarine and sauté the mushrooms for 5 minutes. Stir in half the brandy and turn off heat.

In a saucepan, dissolve the gelatin in the white wine. Bring to a boil, stir, then pour into food processor and puree the chicken and vegetable mixture, adding the remaining brandy, for 2 minutes or until smooth.

Line a 9 × 5-inch loaf pan with 2 overlapping sheets of waxed paper. Spread a layer of mushrooms on the bottom. Spoon puree over mushrooms, forming a second layer. Add chicken pieces to form a third layer. Then spread rest of puree, and top with remaining mushrooms. Fold waxed paper over top and place a couple cans on top to weight it down. Refrigerate overnight.

To unmold, remove weights, unfold waxed paper, and place an inverted serving platter on top. Invert pâté onto platter. Garnish with parsley sprigs and serve with crisp, warmed French bread. (*Serves 8.*)

Note: Since I make a lot of pâtés and terrines, I use an ordinary building brick to compact the pâté. Wrap it in a plastic bag and place it on top of the waxed paper.

Endive Tart

*M*any people think of Belgian endive only as a great ingredient for salads, but braised endive is one of the delicacies of the world. Instead of serving them as an accompaniment, I turn them into a main course. Use any margarine-based pie crust, although here I use filo dough, because it has less fat. This tart serves eight.

    1 to 2 teaspoons olive oil,
            approximately
        6 sheets filo dough
        4 large Belgian endive, trimmed
            and cut in half lengthwise
        6 tablespoons polyunsaturated
            margarine
          Juice of ½ lemon
     1½ tablespoon cornstarch
        1 cup chicken stock
        2 tablespoons skim milk
       ½ teaspoon freshly grated nutmeg
       ½ teaspoon black pepper
        2 tablespoons bread crumbs
        2 tablespoons wheat germ
        1 ounce Swiss cheese, grated

Preheat the oven to 375°F. Brush the bottom of a 10-inch pie pan or Pyrex dish with olive oil. Place 1 sheet of filo dough in the pan, and brush lightly with a few drops of oil. Repeat for each filo sheet. Filo sheets will overhang the pan, so roll them up to fit the perimeter.

Bake for 20 minutes, or until dough is golden brown. Remove.

Meanwhile, bring about 2 cups of water to a boil in a kettle. Blanch the endive for 5 minutes, then drain. In a large skillet, melt 4 tablespoons margarine and braise endive over medium heat for 10 minutes, covered. Endive should be light brown. Add lemon juice.

In a saucepan, melt the remaining 4 tablespoons margarine, add cornstarch, and gradually stir in chicken stock and milk. Cook for 3 minutes, stirring, until sauce thickens. Season with nutmeg and black pepper. Spread cream sauce in pie crust, then place endive on top. Mix the bread crumbs, wheat germ, and cheese, then sprinkle over endive. Trickle remaining oil over topping. Bake for 20 minutes. (*Serves 8.*)

Mâche and Beet Salad with Walnuts

        2 cups mâche (or 1 bunch watercress
            if unavailable)
        2 cooked beets, sliced, or 1 can (1
            pound) sliced beets
       ¼ cup walnuts
        1 tablespoon Dijon-style mustard
        3 tablespoons walnut oil
          Juice of 1 lemon
          Salt and pepper

In a salad bowl, combine mâche, beets, and walnuts. Stir together mustard, oil, and lemon juice. Pour over salad and toss. Season to taste with salt and pepper.

Cantaloupe Sorbet

1 *very ripe cantaloupe or musk
   melon*
1 *cup water*
⅓ *cup granulated sugar*
  Juice of 2 limes
⅓ *cup confectioners' sugar*
2 *egg whites, beaten until stiff*
1 *dozen ladyfingers*
8 *mint leaves*
4 *strawberries, for decoration
   (optional)*

Scoop out melon. (Even if your melon is over-ripe, don't worry: even if it's too ripe to eat, it can still be fine for sorbet.) In a saucepan, combine water and granulated sugar, then cook over medium heat for about 10 minutes, until syrupy. Chill. (Syrup can be prepared a day ahead.)

In a blender or food processor, puree melon, adding lime juice and sugar syrup. Pour into a metal bowl and freeze for 30 minutes.

In a separate bowl, fold confectioners' sugar into egg whites. Place this bowl in a pan of boiling water, and cook for 10 minutes, or until mixture becomes firm but softer than a meringue. Freeze for 30 minutes.

Combine contents of both bowls with a spoon or fork until thoroughly mixed. Freeze for at least 2 hours.

On each dessert plate, place 3 ladyfingers, top with a scoop of sorbet, then decorate with 2 mint leaves and a strawberry.

Note: This is an old-fashioned way of making sorbet. You may prefer to use an ice-cream machine. The ingredients remain the same, but follow the manufacturer's instructions for freezing.

	Calories	Cholesterol (mg)	Total Fat (g)	Saturated Fat (g)	Sodium (mg)
A Safe and Light Pâté of Mushrooms and Chicken	224	42	26.6	5.2	397
Endive Tart	155	3	11.8	3.0	253
Mâche and Beet Salad with Walnuts	271	—	14.5	1.4	165
Cantaloupe Sorbet	213	—	2.0	—	25
TOTAL	863	45	54.9	9.6	840
% of Total Calories			57	10	

* *Note:* Quantities given indicate nutritional value per serving.

Menu

22

Gazpacho

Mussels à l'Escargot Jeannette

Hearts of Escarole Salad

Plum and Peach Compote

One of the advantages of this menu is that it can be entirely prepared ahead of time. It is light, delicious, and healthful. For those who may wonder, "Gazpacho in winter?" be assured that thousands of Spanish gourmets find it a welcome course throughout the year.

Gazpacho

For the soup

½ loaf day-old French bread, soaked in water and squeezed dry

1 (1-pound) can whole tomatoes

1 large green bell pepper, cored, peeled (with a potato peeler), and cut into chunks

1½ cucumbers, peeled and cut in 1-inch slices

1 large onion, quartered

½ cup wine vinegar

¼ cup olive oil

Juice of 1 lemon

1 to 2 teaspoons Tabasco or to taste

3 cups chicken stock or water

For the garnish

½ cucumber, peeled and diced

1 tomato, diced

1 green bell pepper, cored, and diced

1 cup finely chopped fresh parsley

In a food processor or blender, puree the soaked bread, tomatoes, green pepper, cucumber, onion, vinegar, oil, lemon juice, and Tabasco. (Since the volume of ingredients exceeds the capacity of a food processor or blender, do this in several batches.) Transfer to a soup tureen and stir with a wooden spoon. Add the chicken stock or water and mix thoroughly.

In a bowl, mix the garnishes. Add half to the soup tureen and refrigerate. The remaining garnishes are passed at the table when soup is served.

Note: Not only can the gazpacho be prepared ahead of time, it is desired for the soup seasons in sitting. In fact, it benefits from up to a week's stay in the refrigerator.

If desired, add or substitute the following garnishes: hard-boiled, chopped egg whites; finely chopped scallions; croutons; and finely chopped lettuce leaves.

Mussels à l'Escargot Jeannette

*F*or those who like the *idea* of snails but balk at the eating, mussels are an acceptable and accessible alternative. Since mussels come in all sizes, cut larger ones in half after they have been steamed. This is a very rich dish—in the tradition of the classic escargot preparation. If the fat content is too high for you, you can substitute a recipe for mussels steamed in white wine, called *moules marinères*. But I hope you can indulge just this once.

  1 cup dry white wine
  1 cup water
  1 teaspoon dried thyme
  1 onion, diced
  24 large or 48 small mussels, well scrubbed and beards removed
  ½ pound polyunsaturated margarine
  1 generous cup chopped fresh parsley
  10 garlic cloves
  2 teaspoons freshly grated nutmeg
  1 teaspoon black pepper
  3 slices whole wheat bread, cut into 2-inch cubes
  ¼ cup brandy
  2 tomatoes, diced fine

In a kettle (3- to 4-quart pot), bring the wine, water, thyme, and onion to a boil. Add the mussels, cover, and steam for 5 minutes, or until all mussels are open. (Stir once or twice with a wooden spoon to circulate heat.)

Meanwhile, in a blender or food processor, puree the margarine, parsley, garlic, nutmeg, pepper, bread cubes, and brandy. Set aside. Preheat the oven to 350°F.

Drain mussels. Discard any that do not open. Place mussels on a board, and with a knife, split in half to separate the shells. (You will need both top and bottom). With absorbent paper, wipe the inside of shells clean.

Place 12 half-shells in each of 4 individual baking dishes (escargot dishes serve the purpose). Place half a large mussel (or 1 whole small mussel) in each shell half, sprinkle with a few tomato cubes, then cover generously with pureed mixture. Bake for 10 minutes, or until tops are bubbling. To serve, put each individual dish on a regular dinner plate. Serve with warm French bread.

Hearts of Escarole Salad

*C*risp, crunchy escarole is a welcome follow-up to the mussels. Since the outer leaves tend to be bitter, use only the hearts.

> 2 *heads escarole, outer leaves removed*
>   *Vinaigrette of your choice (page xviii)*

Place leaves in a large salad bowl, pour over the dressing, and toss well.

Plum and Peach Compote

*L*ike the gazpacho, the fragrance of this dessert is enhanced as it seasons and it, too, can be kept for up to a week, refrigerated.

> 3 *cups water*
> 1½ *cups sugar*
> 4 *ripe peaches*
> 4 *ripe plums*
> 1 *tablespoon vanilla extract*

In a kettle, bring the water and sugar to a boil. Reduce heat to medium and cook for 10 to 15 minutes, or until liquid becomes syrupy. Add the fruit and simmer for 5 minutes. Turn off heat, add vanilla, and let cool.

When cool, peel fruit, halve and place back in syrup. Refrigerate, covered.

	Calories	Cholesterol (mg)	Total Fat (g)	Saturated Fat (g)	Sodium (mg)
Gazpacho	258	—	13.5	1.8	455
Mussels à l'Escargot Jeannette	710	25	45.6	8.4	105
Hearts of Escarole Salad	45	—	—	—	200
Plum and Peach Compote	209	—	—	—	—
TOTAL	1,222	25	59.1	10.2	760
% of Total Calories			44	8	

* Note: Quantities given indicate nutritional value per serving.

Menu

23

Baked Eggplant with Garlic

Grilled Breast of Turkey Steaks
with Provençal Herbs

New Potatoes with Parsley

Cold Apple Soufflé
with an Apricot Coulis

Baked Eggplant with Garlic

Many ethnic cuisines use eggplant in their own special way. It is one of the staples of Middle Eastern cuisine, which features it as an hors d'oeuvre, as a main course, and as a salad. It is also inspiration for an infinite variety of Indian dishes, as well as those of Italy and the south of France. In areas where the price and paucity of meat are legendary, eggplant lends itself—through its rich consistency and flavor—to countless dishes that are essentially meat substitutes. This recipe is French, and very elegant. In addition, the garlic and eggplant constitute a formidable anti-cholesterol duo. If at all possible, look for small eggplants (4 to 6 inches long), although the larger ones will do.

> 6 garlic cloves, slivered, plus 1
>   tablespoon minced garlic
> ½ cup olive oil
> 1½ teaspoons dried thyme
> ½ teaspoon dried oregano
> ½ teaspoon dried ground sage

> ½ teaspoon dried tarragon
> ½ teaspoon dried rosemary
> ½ teaspoon freshly ground black
>   pepper
> 4 small whole eggplants
> ½ cup finely chopped fresh parsley

Preheat the oven to 400°F. In a bowl, mix the slivered garlic with the olive oil, dried herbs, and pepper. Let marinate for 15 minutes.

With the tip of a sharp knife, prick the eggplants with ½-inch slits. Insert garlic slivers in each slot, then brush eggplant thoroughly with oil marinade. Wrap eggplants individually in foil and place side by side in an ovenproof dish. Bake for 30 to 40 minutes.

Unwrap eggplants and place on a platter. Slit open lengthwise and pour in any remaining marinade. Sprinkle the minced garlic and parsley over, and serve.

Note: As an alternative, 1 large eggplant rather than several small, and proceed as described. Bring whole eggplant to the table and slice it as you would a roast.

Grilled Breast of Turkey Steaks
with Provençal Herbs

•

*T*urkey meat is somewhat heartier than chicken, and in this recipe I use it to achieve a veal-chop quality. Buy a whole breast of turkey, and have it sliced into inch-thick steaks. Turkey has about 30 percent less cholesterol than veal, and from a culinary viewpoint it is a most honorable substitute.

Juice of ½ lemon
1 tablespoon Provençal Herbs
4 turkey steaks

Prepare grill or preheat the broiler. Sprinkle lemon juice and the Provençal Herbs (a mixture of thyme, rosemary, sage leaf, bay leaf, and basil) over turkey and let stand for 10 minutes. Grill the turkey for about 10 minutes on each side. Serve with New Poratoes with Parsley (page 60).

Cold Apple Soufflé
with an Apricot Coulis

•

For the soufflé

4 tart apples
Rind of 1 lemon, cut in thin strips
1 tablespoon unflavored gelatin
¼ cup cold water

Juice of 1 lemon
2 tablespoons sugar
2 egg whites, beaten until stiff
Few mint leaves, for garnish

For the coulis

12 dried apricots, reconstituted in water, and drained
1 teaspoon vanilla extract
2 tablespoons sugar

Preheat the oven to 400°F. Pour ½ inch of cold water into a medium baking dish. Put in apples and bake for 40 minutes.

In a saucepan, bring about 1 cup of water to a boil, and simmer lemon rind for 15 minutes. Drain.

Dissolve gelatin in cold water, then place in a saucepan, bring to a boil, and turn off heat.

Slice off tops of apples and reserve. Scoop out pulp, discarding core and seeds. In a blender, puree apple pulp, gelatin, lemon juice and lemon rind, and sugar. Fold in egg whites. Fill apple shells with puree, then place tops. Refrigerate for at least 1 to 2 hours. Decorate with mint leaves.

In a blender, puree the ingredients for coulis. Pour into a serving bowl. Spoon a dollop over each soufflé and pass the rest at serving time.

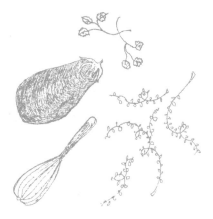

	Calories	Cholesterol (mg)	Total Fat (g)	Saturated Fat (g)	Sodium (mg)
Baked Eggplant with Garlic	300	—	27.0	3.6	—
Grilled Breast of Turkey Steaks with Provençal Herbs	170	76	5.0	1.6	70
New Potatoes	120	—	—	—	6
Cold Apple Soufflé with an Apricot Coulis	162	—	—	—	25
TOTAL	987	76	45.5	7.0	101
% of Total Calories			41	6	

* *Note:* Quantities given indicate nutritional value per serving.

One-Eyed Omelette with Herbs and Mushrooms

Crostini with Anchoyade

Arugula Salad with Oranges and Red Onions

Upside-Down Plum Cake

One-Eyed Omelette with Herbs and Mushrooms

*D*espite the dietary restrictions imposed on us, my husband and I had no intention of foregoing the pleasure of omelettes. How to accomplish this? With the omission—or near omission—of yolks. This recipe uses a single yolk, and since it serves four people, that adds up to only a quarter-yolk per person. Even the strictest doctor could not take umbrage at that, or so I reasoned.

6 *egg whites*
1 *egg yolk*
1 *tablespoon nonfat powdered milk*
  Fresh pepper to taste
½ *cup finely chopped fresh chives*
½ *cup finely chopped fresh parsley*

3 *tablespoons polyunsaturated*
  margarine
1 *cup sliced button mushrooms*
  Sprigs of parsley, for garnish

In a mixing bowl, beat the egg whites, yolk, powdered milk, pepper, and herbs.

In a skillet, melt the margarine and cook the mushrooms for 3 minutes over low heat. Pour egg mixture into skillet and cook. After 1 minute, gently lift omelette with a fork, tilting pan to allow remaining liquid to flow underneath and cook. Continue cooking until omelette looks firm while top remains moist. Fold in half with a spatula and place on a serving platter. Garnish with parsley sprigs.

Note: For those for whom even one yolk is too many, substitute 3 ounces tofu for the egg yolk.

Crostini with Anchoyade

·

8 *thick slices whole wheat bread*
¼ *cup olive oil*
2 *garlic cloves, minced*
1 *(2-ounce) can anchovy filets*
  Juice of ½ lemon
1 *cup finely chopped fresh parsley*

Toast the bread. Pour olive oil and half the garlic over the slices. In a blender or food processor, puree the anchovies and remaining garlic, together with the lemon juice and half the parsley. Spread mixture over bread. Sprinkle with remaining parsley.

Arugula Salad with Oranges and Red Onions

·

1 *bunch arugula, trimmed*
1 *red onion, sliced*
1 *orange, peeled and sliced*
  Vinaigrette of your choice (page xviii)

Place arugula in a salad bowl and top with the onion and orange. Serve with vinaigrette.

Upside-Down Plum Cake

·

6 *tablespoons polyunsaturated margarine*
⅔ *cup sugar*
1 *teaspoon ground cinnamon*
1 *pound plums, cut into eighths*
2 *egg whites*
1 *cup unbleached all-purpose flour*
½ *teaspoon freshly grated nutmeg*
1 *tablespoon almond extract*
1 *tablespoon rum or kirsch*
⅓ *cup skim milk*
1 *teaspoon baking powder*
1 *cup nonfat vanilla yogurt*

Preheat the oven to 375°F. Melt 2 tablespoons margarine and use to coat an 8-inch square baking dish. Sprinkle 2 tablespoons sugar and half the cinnamon on the bottom of the dish. Place plums in dish.

In a mixing bowl, cream remaining margarine and sugar. Add egg whites, flour, nutmeg, extract, rum, and milk. Add baking powder last, otherwise it will prevent leavening. Pour batter over plums and bake for 30 minutes.

Let cake stand 10 minutes, then place serving platter over dish. Invert cake onto platter. Serve warm with yogurt. (*Serves 8.*)

The (Almost) No Cholesterol Gourmet Cookbook

	Calories	Cholesterol (mg)	Total Fat (g)	Saturated Fat (g)	Sodium (mg)
One-Eyed Omelette with Herbs and Mushrooms	139	68	9.9	2.2	197
Crostini with Anchoyade	360	—	15.0	1.8	375
Arugula Salad with Oranges and Red Onions	35	—	—	—	—
Upside-Down Plum Cake	241	—	9.1	1.6	181
TOTAL	775	68	34.0	5.6	753
% Total Calories			39	7	

* *Note:* Quantities given indicate nutritional value per serving.

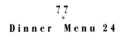

Menu

25

Asparagus Vinaigrette with White Mimosa

Cold Bluefish Filets with Anise Sauce

Red Potato Salad

Chilled Haricot Verts Salad

Raspberry, Blackberry, and Strawberry Charlotte with Raspberry Coulis

This entirely cold menu is especially welcome in warm weather. But it is also ideal for a late-night after-theater dinner, served with Champagne.

Asparagus Vinaigrette with White Mimosa

·

When I grew up, in France, one of the wonderful harbingers of spring was white asparagus. White asparagus is relatively rare and difficult to find outside of France. I have used green asparagus, which is readily available and almost as delicious. The classic mimosa preparation uses the full egg; here we get the same elegant effect with only the white.

For the asparagus

20 asparagus, peeled and trimmed
1 bunch fresh parsley, finely chopped
4 hard-boiled egg whites, finely chopped

For the vinaigrette

2 tablespoons balsamic vinegar
1 large teaspoon Dijon-style mustard
7 tablespoons olive oil
   Ground black pepper

In a kettle, steam the asparagus for 8 minutes. (If you do not have a steamer, improvise by using a saucepan and a steaming basket.) Place 5 asparagus on each plate, then sprinkle a row of parsley and a row of mimosa across each. Prepare the vinaigrette by blending ingredients well, then pour over asparagus.

Cold Bluefish Filets
with an Anise Sauce

·

Juice of ½ lemon
4 bluefish filets
1 lemon, cut in slices
Fresh pepper to taste

Preheat the oven to 350°F. Spoon the lemon juice over the filets, then place them in a large baking dish, cover with lemon slices. Sprinkle with pepper. Seal with foil. Bake for 10 minutes, then let cool for roughly 30 minutes. Refrigerate, covered, until serving time.

For the sauce

1 fennel bulb, trimmed and cut in
  chunks
2 slices white bread
4 hard-boiled egg whites
  Juice of 1 lemon
½ cup olive oil
1 tablespoon Pernod
  Fresh pepper to taste

For the decoration

1 cucumber, unpeeled and sliced
1 lemon, sliced
  Few sprigs of dill

In a food processor or blender, puree the sauce ingredients. Thin the sauce with water if you find it's too thick. Remove fish from refrigerator, spoon anise sauce over filets, and decorate with cucumber, lemon, and dill.

Red Potato Salad

·

2 pounds large red new potatoes,
  scrubbed and cut in quarters (if
  small, leave whole)
1 heaping tablespoon Dijon-style
  mustard
½ cup plain 1% yogurt
6 tablespoons olive oil
2 tablespoons balsamic vinegar
1 green bell pepper, diced
5 scallions, trimmed and chopped
  Fresh pepper
  Few sprigs of dill

In a kettle, bring about 2 quarts of water to a boil and cook potatoes for 12 to 15 minutes, or until tender. Drain.

Place warm potatoes in a large serving bowl and add mustard, yogurt, oil, vinegar, pepper, and scallions. Toss and adjust seasoning to taste. Let cool, then serve, garnished with dill.

Note: Do not be concerned if potatoes crumble and do not remain intact. Your salad will be just as good, and actually have a special charm.

Chilled Haricot Verts Salad

·

1 pound thin green beans
  Lemon Vinaigrette (page xviii)

Steam beans until they are just tender. Immediately plunge them into cold water to set their color. Chill until serving time, then toss with the vinaigrette.

Raspberry, Blackberry, and Strawberry Charlotte with Raspberry Coulis

•

2 dozen ladyfingers
¾ cup sugar
3 tablespoons water
1 pint fresh raspberries
1 pint fresh blackberries
1 pint fresh strawberries
1 pound low-fat vanilla yogurt

Moisten the bottom and sides of a charlotte mold with margarine or peanut oil. (If you do not have a charlotte mold, use a medium-size mixing bowl with a high rim.) Cut ladyfingers lengthwise, reserving a few for the top, and line bottom and sides of bowl.

In a saucepan, melt the sugar in the water, then bring to a boil. Reduce heat and add half the raspberries. After 1 minute, remove the raspberries with a slotted spoon. Set aside and reserve juice. Repeat process with *all* the blackberries and strawberries.

On the ladyfinger base, place a layer of cooked raspberries, followed by a layer of blackberries, then of strawberries. Spread ½ cup of yogurt on top of strawberries. Repeat process until fruit is used up. Cover with reserved ladyfingers and seal with plastic wrap. Chill overnight in refrigerator.

In a saucepan, bring the reserved berry juices to a boil. Add the remaining raspberries, reduce the heat, and cook until syrupy. Puree in a blender, then set aside to cool.

At serving time, place a serving platter over the charlotte mold and invert charlotte onto platter. Cover top of charlotte with remaining yogurt, and top with sauce. (*Serves 8.*)

Note: If blackberries are unavailable, substitute with blueberries.

	Calories	Cholesterol (mg)	Total Fat (g)	Saturated Fat (g)	Sodium (mg)
Asparagus Vinaigrette with White Mimosa	229	—	20.3	2.7	193
Cold Bluefish Filets with Anise Sauce	693	67	31.8	3.6	231
Red Potato Salad	598	—	14.0	2.3	163
Chilled Haricot Verts Salad	136	—	10.1	1.4	4
Raspberry, Blackberry, and Strawberry Charlotte with Raspberry Coulis	249	—	3.3	—	—
TOTAL	1,905	67	79.5	10	591
% of Total Calories			38	6	

* *Note:* Quantities given indicate nutritional value per serving.

•
The (Almost) No Cholesterol Gourmet Cookbook

Menu

26

Grilled Endive with Lemon and Olive Oil

Linguine in Black Olive and Lemon Sauce

Green Salad Saisonière

Cold Soup of Apples, Raspberries, Blackberries, and Oranges

This menu is as delectable as it is relatively easy to prepare and healthful. Olive oil not only lacks cholesterol but has been shown to lower LDL and raise HDL levels in the bloodstream. Here we have olive oil in both the hors d'oeuvre and the main course. A fresh fruit soup rounds out the meal, making this a paragon of menus.

Grilled Endive with Lemon and Olive Oil

4 Belgian endive, halved lengthwise
4 tablespoons olive oil
Juice of ½ lemon
Freshly ground pepper

Prepare grill or preheat broiler. In a kettle, bring about 1 quart water to a boil and blanch the endive for 5 minutes. Drain well by squeezing out water with a fork over a colander. Brush endive lightly and evenly with olive oil on both sides. Grill or broil the endives for 5 to 6 minutes on each side, or until they are tender. Pour remaining olive oil and lemon juice over endive, sprinkle with pepper to taste, and serve.

Linguine in a Black Olive and Lemon Sauce

Rind of 1 lemon, julienned
½ pound Italian black olives, pitted and chopped
Juice of ½ lemon
1 pound linguini, preferably fresh
3 tablespoons olive oil
½ cup finely chopped fresh parsley
Freshly ground pepper to taste

In a small saucepan, bring about 1 cup of water to a boil. Cook lemon rind for 5 minutes, then drain and set aside.

Reserve a couple tablespoons of olives for decoration. Puree remaining olives, together with lemon juice and lemon rind, in a food processor.

Cook linguine until al dente (5 minutes for fresh) and drain. Rinse under cold water and drain again. In a large saucepan, heat the olive oil, and parsley, then stir in linguini. In a separate saucepan, heat the pureed olives and lemon rind. Transfer linguine to a serving platter, pour olive sauce over linguine, and top with reserved chopped olives. Sprinkle pepper over and serve.

Green Salad Saisonière

*S*alad is always welcome after a pasta main course. Use arugula if it's in season, mixed with radicchio and red leaf or Boston lettuce, in keeping with the Italian overtones of this menu. And, of course, use olive oil in your dressing!

1 bunch arugula
A few leaves radicchio
A few leaves red leaf salad or Boston lettuce
Vinaigrette of your choice (page xviii)

In a salad bowl, combine greens, toss with the vinaigrette. Serve.

The (Almost) No Cholesterol Gourmet Cookbook

Cold Soup of Apples, Raspberries, Blackberries, and Oranges

*F*resh fruit is always best for this recipe, but in the event you cannot find fresh berries, substitute frozen berries. This aromatic, light, and refreshing dessert could easily be offered as the conclusion to any meal in this book.

4 cups water

1½ cups sugar

Rind of 1 lemon, cut in strips

Rind of 1 orange, cut in strips

1 tablespoon vanilla extract

2 apples, cored and finely sliced

1 cup fresh raspberries

1 cup fresh blackberries

1 orange, peeled, seeded, and sliced

In a saucepan, bring water, sugar, and both rinds to a boil. Reduce heat to medium and cook for 10 minutes, or until liquid becomes syrupy. Add the vanilla, turn off heat, and let syrup cool. Transfer syrup to a serving bowl, add the fruit, and refrigerate for at least 2 hours. Serve chilled.

	Calories	Cholesterol (mg)	Total Fat (g)	Saturated Fat (g)	Sodium (mg)
Grilled Endive with Lemon and Olive Oil	70	—	6.8	0.9	—
Linguini in Black Olive and Lemon Sauce	399	—	22.1	2.7	100
Green Salad Saisonière	130	—	13.5	1.8	—
Cold Soup of Apples, Raspberries, Blackberries, and Oranges	352	—	—	—	—
TOTAL	951	0	42.4	5.4	100
% of Total Calories			40	5	

* *Note:* Quantities given indicate nutritional value per serving.

Menu

27

Brochette of Chicken with Hot Peanut Sauce

Skewered Vegetables

**Salad of Red and Green Cabbage
with Sesame Dressing**

Glazed Oranges in Grand Marnier Syrup

This very light oriental menu can be prepared either indoors or out depending on the season and your facilities. A charcoal grill and your oven broiler give slightly different but equally satisfying results.

Brochette of Chicken

·

4 *chicken breasts (each about 12 ounces), skin removed, cut into 1-inch pieces*

8 *tablespoons polyunsaturated margarine*

¼ *cup low-sodium soy sauce*
 Juice of 2 limes

1 *teaspoon crushed coriander seed*

½ *cup finely chopped fresh coriander (cilantro)*
 Hot Peanut Sauce (recipe follows)

If grilling, prepare the coals. Spear the chicken pieces on 4 skewers and place on a deep platter. In a saucepan, melt the margarine, then add the soy sauce, lime juice, and crushed coriander. Brush sauce on all sides of chicken and pour over. Marinate for roughly 30 minutes, then grill over hot coals or broil 3 inches from the heat, turning the skewers until chicken is golden brown, about 20 minutes. Sprinkle with fresh coriander and serve with peanut sauce. (This is also nice served over brown rice.)

Hot Peanut Sauce

I've included the Hot Peanut Sauce here because it's delicious. However, if you find its fat content too high, you can make the sauce without the peanut butter, peanuts, boiling water and still have a light and piquant sauce.

- 1 tablespoon peanut oil
- 1 medium onion, chopped
- 2 garlic cloves, minced
- ⅔ cup peanut butter
- 1 teaspoon grated fresh ginger
- 1 fresh red chili pepper, or ½ teaspoon cayenne pepper
- 1 tablespoon soy sauce
- 2 tablespoons lime juice
- 1 cup finely chopped fresh parsley
- ⅓ cup boiling water
- ½ cup coarsely chopped unsalted peanuts

In a skillet, heat the oil and sauté the onion and garlic until light brown. Transfer to a blender and puree with next 6 ingredients. Return to saucepan and add boiling water. Keep warm over low heat. (*Note:* If sauce becomes too thick, add a trifle more boiling water.)

When ready to serve, transfer sauce to a serving bowl and sprinkle on the chopped peanuts.

Skewered Vegetables

- 1 cup fresh oregano, or 1 tablespoon dried
- ¼ cup oriental sesame oil
  Fresh pepper
- 2 small zucchinis, trimmed and cut in ½-inch slices
- 2 small yellow squash, trimmed and cut in ½-inch slices
- 2 red onions, cut in thick slices

If grilling, prepare coals. In a bowl, mix the oregano, oil, and pepper. Add the vegetable slices and marinate for 10 minutes. Spear vegetables on 4 skewers, then grill or broil for about 3 to 5 minutes on both sides for al dente, slightly longer for better done. Baste with marinade to moisten vegetables while they cook.

Salad of Red and Green Cabbage with Sesame Dressing

- 1 small red cabbage, outer leaves discarded and inner shredded
- 1 small green cabbage, outer leaves discarded and inner shredded
- ½ cup sesame oil
- 3 tablespoons rice or distilled white vinegar
- ½ cup finely chopped fresh coriander (cilantro)
  Fresh pepper to taste

Combine ingredients, chill, and serve.

Glazed Oranges in
Grand Marnier Syrup

*

*T*his cool and refreshing dessert is especially well suited to the otherwise spicy meal. While light, its elegance adds a gala touch to the meal.

4 to 6 seedless oranges
⅔ cup water
1 cup sugar
Juice of 1 lemon
⅔ cup Grand Marnier

With a sharp knife, remove the zest from the oranges (not the white layer) and julienne. Combine water, sugar, and lemon juice in a saucepan. Bring to a boil and reduce heat, then add zest and cook for 15 minutes, until syrup is thick. Turn off heat and add Grand Marnier. Let cool.

Using a sharp knife, remove all vestiges of white membrane from orange. (Do this over a bowl to catch the juice.) Still holding oranges over the bowl, cut crosswise into thin slices. Reassemble the orange slices to look like an orange onto a serving dish. Pour the orange juice from the bowl into the syrup and stir. Spoon syrup over oranges and decorate each orange with caramelized peel. Refrigerate.

	Calories	Cholesterol (mg)	Total Fat (g)	Saturated Fat (g)	Sodium (mg)
Brochette of Chicken with Hot Peanut Sauce	1,111	93	98.0	14.9	1,403
Recipe with light sauce	754	93	67.4	10.1	1,053
Skewered Vegetables	160	—	13.6	1.9	—
Salad of Red and Green Cabbage with Sesame Dressing	300	—	27.2	3.8	—
Glazed Oranges in Grand Marnier Syrup	316	—	—	—	—
TOTAL	1,887	93	138.8	20.6	1,403
% of Total Calories			66	10	
TOTAL (with light sauce)	1,530	93	108.2	15.8	1,153
% of Total Calories			64	9	

* *Note:* Quantities given indicate nutritional value per serving.

Menu

28

Quail and Black Truffles on Canapés, Served with Marmalade of Leeks

Belgian Endive with Walnuts

Miniature Coffee and Chocolate Eclairs

*U*ntil recently quail was synonymous with what is esoteric and elegant, in the ranks of caviar. Today quail are much more available, either fresh at local butchers or frozen in supermarkets. Yet for entertaining, quail remains a delicacy and makes a lasting impression.

This menu is a slight digression from the relatively sinless meals, in that dark meat is not as low in cholesterol as white meat. Still, like quail itself, the sin here is small.

Quail and Black Truffles on Canapés, Served with Marmalade of Leeks

For the quail

6 *tablespoons olive oil*

8 *quail, skins off*

½ *cup beef broth*

12 *slices canned black truffles, with juices*

3 *tablespoons Madeira*

1 *tablespoon brandy*

For the canapés

2 *generous tablespoons olive oil*

8 *slices whole grain bread*

½ *cup finely chopped fresh parsley*

Preheat the oven to 350°F. In a skillet, heat the olive oil, reduce heat to medium, and brown the quail on all sides for no more than 10 to 12 minutes. Place birds in a medium baking dish and pour half the pan juices over them. Cover with foil and bake for 20 minutes.

In the same skillet, reheat the remaining pan juices, add the broth, then reduce heat to a simmer. Add the truffle slices in their juice and simmer for 1 more minute. Pour in Madeira and brandy, ignite, let the flames subside, and then stir. Set aside.

In a skillet, heat the oil for the canapes and fry bread slices on both sides. Drain. Place fried bread on a serving platter and rest a quail on each slice. Sprinkle the parsley over the quail and dress each quail with a truffle slice or two and top with some truffle sauce. Serve with Leek Marmalade.

Marmalade of Leeks

*P*repare the marmalade first, so you can simply reheat it for 5 minutes before serving.

> 8 *to 10 leeks, trimmed and washed*
> *well*
> ¾ *cup chicken stock*
> 2 *tablespoons olive oil or*
> *polyunsaturated margarine*
> ½ *cup finely chopped fresh parsley*
> *Fresh pepper and salt to taste*

Cut leeks in 1-inch pieces. Put leeks and stock in a kettle and bring to a boil. Reduce heat and simmer for about 10 minutes, or until soft. Pour leeks and liquid into a food processor or blender and puree.

Return to kettle, heat the oil or margarine then add the pureed leeks and the parsley. Cook over very low heat for 15 minutes, stirring constantly until most of the liquid has evaporated. Season to taste, and serve either on a separate platter or around your canapes.

Belgian Endive with Walnuts

> 1 *tablespoon sherry vinegar*
> 3 *tablespoons walnut or olive oil*
> *Fresh pepper and salt*
> 6 *to 7 Belgian endive, leaves*
> *separated, immersed in cold water,*
> *and drained*
> ½ *cup shelled walnuts*

Prepare dressing of vinegar, oil, and seasonings in a salad bowl. Put in endive leaves and top with walnuts. Toss.

Miniature Coffee and Chocolate Eclairs

*T*hroughout France, *boulangerie-patisseries*, however small, feature the country's classic pastry—the eclair—either chocolate or coffee flavor. I have often enjoyed making miniature eclairs for dessert, but their richness dictated that I serve them only after light meals. When the cholesterol alert rang, I knew I could never even dream of making eclairs. But not wanting to admit defeat, I started experimenting until, one day, I found just what I had hoped for: an eclair *without yolks, without butter, without cream, without real coffee.* (I even made them without sugar for a diabetic friend . . . but I won't go into that here.) Having eliminated all the prime ingredients that make the charm and raison d'être of eclairs, what, might you ask, is there left? The fact is, my new eclairs not only look like the original, but, more to the point, taste like them, too.

For the pastry

> 8 *tablespoons soy butter or*
> *polyunsaturated margarine*
> 1 *cup water*
> 1 *cup unbleached all-purpose flour*
> 6 *egg whites*

Preheat the oven to 375°F. In a saucepan set over medium heat, melt soy butter or margarine in the water. Bring to a boil, remove from heat, and rapidly stir in flour to form a thick dough. Add egg whites and continue stirring until you have a smooth, thick, pastelike dough.

Put 2 or 3 spoonfuls of dough into a pastry tube. Squeeze dough out of the pastry tube onto a baking sheet to form thin cylinders about 2 inches long. Continue until all the dough is used, placing cylinders side by side on the sheet. Bake for 25 to 30 minutes, or until cylinders have puffed up, are golden, and are no longer sticky. Let cool briefly, then with a small serrated knife, gently slice off top of each eclair. Set aside.

For the chocolate custard

2 ounces unsweetened chocolate
1½ cups vanilla soy milk
2 tablespoons cornstarch
3 tablespoons granulated sugar

In a saucepan over low heat, melt the chocolate with 3 tablespoons of soy milk. Stir in cornstarch and gradually pour remaining milk and the sugar, stirring until it thickens to custard consistency. Taste for sweetness, and adjust according to your taste. Let cool.

For the coffee custard

2 tablespoons instant decaffeinated coffee
2 tablespoons cornstarch
1½ cups vanilla soy milk
2 tablespoons granulated sugar

In a saucepan, mix the coffee and cornstarch with 3 tablespoons soy milk. Place over low heat and stir in remaining soy milk and the sugar. Continue stirring until mixture thickens to custard consistency. Taste and adjust for sweetness. Let cool.

For the chocolate icing

1 ounce unsweetened chocolate, melted with 1 tablespoon soy milk
1 cup confectioners' sugar
1 teaspoon soy milk

In a bowl, mix all ingredients for chocolate icing to form a thick paste. (If too thick, add a few more drops soy milk; if too liquid, add more confectioners' sugar.) Cover and set aside.

For the coffee icing

1 tablespoon instant decaffeinated coffee
2 tablespoons soy milk
1 cup confectioners' sugar

In a bowl, dissolve coffee in soy milk. Stir in sugar, then cover and set aside.

To assemble the eclairs, use a couple of teaspoons to fill the eclair bottoms with custard, half with chocolate, half with coffee. Take half the cut-off caps and place them on a plate. With a teaspoon, spread chocolate icing over the caps, coating them generously. Allow to set for a few minutes. Repeat for remaining caps, using coffee icing. Place iced caps over filled bottoms. Serve eclairs on a large platter lined with a lace doily. Should there be leftover eclairs, wrap them well and refrigerate. They will be good for several days.

	Calories	Cholesterol (mg)	Total Fat (g)	Saturated Fat (g)	Sodium (mg)
Quail and Black Truffles on Canapés Served with Marmalade of Leeks	783	110	39.5	6.2	503
Belgian Endive with Walnuts	215	—	18.8	1.4	145
Miniature Eclairs	354	—	13.3	2.1	193
TOTAL	1,352	110	71.6	9.7	841
% of Total Calories			41	6	

* *Note:* Quantities given indicate nutritional value per serving.

The (Almost) No Cholesterol Gourmet Cookbook

Menu

29

Cream of Lemon Soup

Artichoke, Celery, and Parsley Tart

Endive Salad with Lemon Dressing

Peach and Raspberry Terrine
with Passion Fruit Sauce

This menu has many virtues: it is exquisite, delicious, exotic, and positively cholesterol free.

Cream of Lemon Soup

Lemons, in addition to their vitamin C, have a natural ability to lower blood cholesterol. This soup, a distant cousin of the Greek *avgolemono*, sports the latter's fragrance and the charm without its eggs and cream.

2 large lemons
5 cups chicken stock

3 tablespoons cream of rice cereal
diluted in 1 cup cold water
Fresh pepper and salt
½ cup finely chopped fresh parsley
½ cup plain low-fat yogurt

With a small, sharp knife, peel 1 lemon. Grate the rind of the second lemon, then squeeze juice from both. Combine stock and lemon juice in a large saucepan. Add peel and rind, and bring to a boil. Reduce heat and simmer for 10 minutes. Pour cereal into pan and cook an additional 10 minutes. Remove and discard lemon peel. Season with pepper and salt. Add parsley and yogurt, then serve.

Artichoke, Celery, and Parsley Tart

*A*rtichokes have many therapeutic qualities, including a tendency to lower blood cholesterol. I developed this recipe after returning from Rome, where I savored *artichoke à la Romana*, or artichoke hearts baked with olive oil and garlic. My variation on that Roman theme is this tart.

    5 artichokes cooked in boiling water
      for 18 minutes and drained
    4 tablespoons olive oil
    2 tablespoons minced shallots
    2 cups finely chopped fresh parsley
      Juice of 1 lemon
    5 sheets filo dough
    3 celery stalks, peeled and sliced
    3 garlic cloves, minced
      Fresh pepper and salt

Preheat the oven to 400°F. Remove leaves from artichokes and reserve for a later hors d'oeuvre. Scrape and discard choke so that you are left only with hearts. Mash 2 of the hearts, coarsely, with a fork. In a skillet, heat 2 tablespoons of the oil and sauté the shallots until light brown. Turn off heat and mix in half the parsley and the two mashed artichoke hearts. Add half the lemon juice and set aside.

In an 8- or 10-inch oiled pie pan, place 1 filo sheet, oil lightly, and place the next sheet over the first. Repeat as above until all sheets are used. Since the sheets will overhang the pan, roll them inward to form a crust around the edge. Bake for 15 to 20 minutes, or until crust is golden brown. Remove from oven and turn oven down to 350°F. Spread crust evenly with artichoke mixture. Slice the remaining 3 artichoke hearts as you would apples for a pie. Pour remaining lemon juice over artichoke slices. Alternate artichoke and celery slices in the crust then add remaining parsley. Sprinkle on garlic, pepper and salt, and dot with remaining oil. Bake for 15 minutes. Serve.

Endive Salad with Lemon Dressing

    4 Belgian endives
      Lemon Vinaigrette (page xviii)

Wash endives. Cut off the base of each endive and separate the leaves. Arrange the leaves on a plate and dress with the vinaigrette.

Peach and Raspberry Terrine with Passion Fruit Sauce

*T*his is an extremely attractive dessert, to both the eye and the palate. It's a novel and elegant way of serving fruit, since it appears on the table like a cake—but without the butter, eggs, flour, or cream.

For the terrine

½ cup bran cereal

1 pint raspberries

1 (3-ounce) package raspberry Jell-O

1¼ cups cold water

3 ripe peaches, peeled and sliced

For the cream

2 tablespoons cornstarch

2 cups soy milk

½ cup sugar

½ cup passion fruit brandy

Line a 9 × 5-inch loaf pan with 2 overlapping sheets of waxed paper. Spread the bran evenly on the bottom. Then add about half the raspberries. Dissolve the Jell-O in ½ cup cold water. Add ¾ cup cold water and heat in a saucepan until it boils. Chill to thicken. Pour one-third of the Jell-O over the raspberries, then arrange peach slices in a second layer. Pour another one-third Jell-O over peaches and form a third layer using remaining raspberries. Cover with remaining Jell-O. Fold waxed paper over top of mold and place in refrigerator for several hours or overnight.

In a small cup, dissolve cornstarch in 2 tablespoons of the soy milk. In a small saucepan, combine cornstarch mixture with remaining soy milk and sugar. Over medium heat, bring to a boil, reduce heat to low, and cook for 2 minutes, stirring well until thickened. Let cool. Stir in brandy and chill.

To unmold terrine, unfold waxed paper, place serving platter over mold, invert, and peel off paper. Slice as you would any terrine or cake, and serve with generous dollops of the cream. (*Serves 8.*)

	Calories	Cholesterol (mg)	Total Fat (g)	Saturated Fat (g)	Sodium (mg)
Cream of Lemon Soup	65	—	0.5	—	1,212
Artichoke, Celery, and Parsley Tart	285	—	17.5	1.8	180
Endive Salad with Lemon Dressing	130	—	13.5	1.8	22
Peach and Raspberry Terrine with Passion Fruit Cream	202	2	1.6	0.2	80
TOTAL	682	2	33.1	3.8	1,494
% of Total Calories			44	7	

* *Note:* Quantities given indicate nutritional value per serving.

Menu

30

Crisp Potato Galette
with Smoked Salmon, Caviar, and
My Sour Cream

Chicken Pot au Feu with Lemon-Dill Sauce

Raspberry Mousse

Cinnamon Almond Macaroons

This gala meal is light, and conforms to our low-cholesterol regime. The small digression is the smoked salmon but, here again, it is offered in small quantity. The chicken is skinned and poached, served with poached vegetables. And as for the seemingly sinful dessert, it's a chaste mousse without cream. The cookies, too, are made without butter or egg yolks.

I feel that the lightness of this pot au feu does not call for a salad course, which is generally an astringent transition to offset a rich main course. But those who feel a meal is incomplete without salad should select one of their choice.

Crisp Potato Galette with Smoked Salmon, Caviar, and My Sour Cream

1 tablespoon olive oil

2 large potatoes, scrubbed clean and shredded

12 ounces low-fat cottage cheese

½ cup finely chopped fresh chives

½ cup chopped fresh dill

½ pound smoked salmon

3 ounces red caviar

In a skillet, heat the oil. Form pancakes from the shredded potatoes by pressing down with a fork. Cook pancakes over medium heat without touching for 8 minutes. Check for crispness by lifting with the fork, and with a spatula, when crisp and golden, flip over to cook on other side. Drain on absorbent paper.

For my sour cream

In a blender or food processor, combine cottage cheese with half the chives and the dill. Blend until cottage cheese is liquefied and smooth.

Place 2 little pancakes *(galettes)* on each plate. Spread with a layer of the chive cream, then some salmon. Cover with another layer of cream. Top with caviar. Sprinkle remaining chives on top.

94

Chicken Pot au Feu
with Lemon-Dill Sauce

1 *chicken, about 5 to 6 pounds, skin removed (or 2 smaller chickens)*

8 *carrots, peeled*

2 *turnips, peeled*

1 *onion stuck with 6 whole cloves*

1 *bunch of celery with leaves, stalks peeled*

½ *bunch fresh dill, or 2 tablespoons dried*

1 *bunch fresh parsley*

1 *tablespoon fresh tarragon*

6 *peppercorns*

½ *teaspoon salt*

3 *leeks, well washed and trimmed*

6 *small new potatoes*

¼ *cup sherry*

For the sauce

1 *tablespoon olive oil*

1 *tablespoon cornstarch*

Juice of 1 lemon

½ *bunch fresh dill, finely chopped*

In a large kettle, place chicken and 3 carrots, the turnips, onion, half the celery (leaves included), the dill, half the parsley, the tarragon, peppercorns, and salt. Add water sufficient to cover by 2 or 3 inches. Bring to a boil, then reduce heat, cover, and simmer for 30 minutes. Transfer chicken to a serving platter (preferably ovenproof), cover, and set aside in a warm oven.

To the kettle, add the remaining carrots, the leeks, potatoes, and remaining celery. Cook for an additional 12 minutes. With a slotted spoon, remove vegetables from kettle and arrange them around the chicken. Recover dish and return to oven to keep warm.

Bring the remaining cooking liquid to a boil, stir in the sherry, and serve piping hot before the chicken and vegetables course. If desired, accompany with warm, crisp French bread. For the main course, bring out the chicken and serve with the sauce on the side.

Prepare the sauce. In a small saucepan, heat the oil, then add the cornstarch, then gradually stir in 1 cup of the cooking liquid until sauce thickens and is smooth. Add the lemon juice and dill. Stir for a minute. Taste and adjust flavor, then transfer to a separate bowl. Keep warm.

Note: Since it takes only 2 or 3 minutes to make the sauce, you can wait to prepare it until after you have served the first course.

Raspberry Mousse

•

1 cup water

½ cup sugar

1 pint fresh raspberries

*1 tablespoon unflavored gelatin,
dissolved in ½ cup water*

¾ cup vanilla soy milk

*1 tablespoon cornstarch, dissolved in
1 tablespoon soy milk*

3 egg whites, beaten until stiff

In a small saucepan, cook water and sugar, over medium heat until syrupy, about 10 minutes. Add the raspberries and continue cooking over low heat, stirring, for 1 more minute.

Press raspberry mixture through a sieve. Add dissolved gelatin and stir. Bring to a boil. Remove from heat.

In a separate saucepan, over low heat, heat the soy milk, adding dissolved cornstarch. Stir until mixture thickens to consistency of custard. Pour into raspberry mixture and stir well. Set aside to chill. When mixture is cold, fold in egg whites. Refrigerate for 3 hours before serving. (*Serves 8.*)

Cinnamon-Almond Macaroons

•

2 cups confectioners' sugar

6 egg whites, beaten until stiff

3 teaspoons ground cinnamon

2 teaspoons grated lemon rind

1 pound almonds, ground

Preheat the oven to 325°F. Gently fold sugar into egg whites. Add cinnamon and lemon rind. Reserve a third of this mixture for later glazing. Gently fold ground almonds into remainder.

On a lightly oiled cookie sheet, drop tablespoonfuls of almond mixture, leaving at least 1 inch between each mound (it will spread on cooking). With a pastry brush or a teaspoon, spread an even layer of the reserved mixture over each cookie. Bake for 20 minutes; cookies will be crisp, not chewy. (*Serves 8.*)

Note: When kept in an airtight container or in the refrigerator, the macaroons will keep a long time.

	Calories	Cholesterol (mg)	Total Fat (g)	Saturated Fat (g)	Sodium (mg)
Crisp Potato Galette with Smoked Salmon, Caviar, and My Sour Cream	307	162	13.0	3.0	662
Chicken Pot au Feu with Lemon-Dill Sauce	448	77	7.9	1.8	343
Raspberry Mousse with Cinnamon-Almond Macaroons	550	—	30.3	2.9	66
TOTAL	1,305	239	51.2	7.7	1,071
% of Total Calories			35	5	

* *Note:* Quantities given indicate nutritional value per serving.

Cream of Celery Root and Potato Soup

Choucroute au Poisson et au Champagne

Pear Sorbet

The centerpiece of this menu is, of course, the choucroute, which is one of the storied dishes of French gastronomy. Although the variant I offer here is extremely light compared to the Alsatian original, it is still sufficiently rich to stand by itself. But try as I may, I cannot rid myself of my traditionalist roots, and I find that the main course is enhanced by a discreet introduction. In fact, what makes French cuisine an art is not only the excellence of each course but the rigor and balance—texture, color, substance, taste—of the totality. In this menu, the exotic vegetable soup is a soothing and delicious opener.

Not many years ago, celery root was virtually unknown and unobtainable. But today it can be found in most supermarkets. Its most famous incarnation is, of course, celery remoulade, one of the staple hors d'oeuvres of France. Celery root has a distinctive and quite wonderful flavor, and when combined with the potato, produces a fragrant and creamy first course.

Cream of Celery Root and Potato Soup

•

2 tablespoons polyunsaturated
   margarine
2 tablespoons flour
1 cup skim milk
2 cups potatoes, peeled and cubed
2 cups celery root, peeled and cubed
½ cup scallions, minced
4 cups vegetable or chicken stock
   Fresh pepper
½ cup fresh parsley, chopped

In a kettle, melt margarine, then add flour and stir in milk. Add potatoes and celery root, scallions, stock, and pepper. Bring to a boil, reduce flame, and cook 15 minutes. Puree, return to kettle. Reheat. Sprinkle parsley and serve. Given the main course of this menu, I suggest serving only a mere cup rather than a full bowl.

Choucroute au Poisson et au Champagne
(Champagne Sauerkraut with Filets of Salmon, Halibut, and Turbot)

*T*he traditional *choucroute alsacienne*, a savory dish consisting of sauerkraut cooked with white wine, spices, and a variety of rich, smoked meats and sausages—the pride of many 4-star restaurants in France—unfortunately ranks among the least recommended dishes for cholesterol watchers. Pork meat and bacon are the prime offenders. With the help and inspiration of a fellow French cook, Catherine, I devised a marvelous variation on the classic theme. I use only a fraction of the bacon required, with absolutely no other pork meats or sausages. Instead, I poach or steam several pieces of fileted fish separately and place them on top of the choucroute, wrapped in a thin and ever so small slice of bacon. This variation of the classic choucroute is every bit as savory, and delicious as the traditional choucroute—but light and cholesterol safe.

2 pounds sauerkraut
2 tablespoons polyunsaturated margarine
2 slices bacon, cut in strips
2 large onions, minced
2 garlic cloves, minced
1 carrot, peeled and thinly sliced
  Few peppercorns
1 cup parsley, finely chopped
1 bay leaf
12 juniper berries
3 to 4 cups Champagne
1 to 2 cups chicken stock
4 slices bacon, blanched for five minutes and drained
1 quarter salmon filet
2 small pieces turbot
1 halibut piece
  Juice of one lemon
½ teaspoon dried tarragon
1 tablespoon scallion or chive, finely chopped
½ teaspoon black pepper
  Few sprigs of parsley for decoration

Preheat the oven to 325°F. Drain sauerkraut and keep under running cold water five minutes. Drain well by squeezing water out with your hands.

In a heavy kettle, melt margarine and the strips of bacon until bacon becomes transluscent. Sauté onion until it too becomes transluscent. Add garlic, carrot, half the parsley, peppercorns, bayleaf, juniper berries, stir 2 minutes. Add sauerkraut, mixing well with ingredients in kettle. Pour in champagne and stock. Top with the 4 bacon slices. Cover tightly and place kettle in oven. Reduce oven heat to 250°F. Bake for 3 to 4 hours. The choucroute should be moist but without liquid.

Cut fish into serving portions about 10 minutes before the choucroute is done, place fish in an ovenproof dish. Pour lemon juice over fish. Top each piece with the tarragon, scallion or chive, and a sprinkling of pepper. Cover tightly with foil, and bake in oven for 8 minutes.

At the time of serving, remove choucroute from oven. With a fork, lift the slices of bacon and set them aside. When fish is cooked, remove foil. With a slotted spoon, place each piece of fish on top of choucroute. Cut bacon slices in half and wrap each piece of fish with the bacon. Intersperse top of choucroute with the fish pieces and boiled potatoes. Sprinkle remaining parsley over potatoes, add parsley sprigs and serve.

This main dish, simmered in wine, plus the lemon juice over the fish, in my view, obviates the need for salad. In fact, moving to the sorbet directly is a light, cleansing and refreshing finale.

Boiled potatoes

Count 2 to 3 new potatoes per person. Cook in boiling water 15 minutes. Drain. Return to pot 2 minutes, stirring in 1 tablespoon olive oil. Add parsley and place on top of choucroute with the fish.

Pear Sorbet

12 ounce can pear nectar

½ cup sugar

4 ripe pears, peeled, cored, and quartered

Juice of 1 lemon

2 egg whites beaten stiff with a pinch of salt

½ cup confectioner's sugar

¾ cup pear brandy, iced in the freezer

In a saucepan, bring to a boil the nectar and the sugar. Reduce to medium flame, cook 10 to 15 minutes or until liquid becomes syrupy. Add pears, cook another 3 minutes. Add lemon juice.

Puree the fruit. Place in a metal bowl and put in the freezer. Allow to set for 1 hour.

In a double boiler over heat mix egg whites with confectioners' sugar. Cook, stirring with a wooden spoon for about 10 minutes. Freeze for about 30 minutes.

Remove both the fruit puree and the "meringue." Combine contents of both into one bowl and return to freezer for a minimum of 4 hours. At serving time, spoon sorbet into serving dishes and top with iced pear brandy. (Serves 8.)

	Calories	Cholesterol (mg)	Total Fat (g)	Saturated Fat (g)	Sodium (mg)
Cream of Celery Root and Potato Soup	220	—	7.4	1.5	365
Choucroute au Poisson et au Champagne	444	49	15.5	3.4	1,135
Boiled Potatoes	130	—	5.9	0.5	8
Pear Sorbet	276	—	0.4	—	15
TOTAL	1,070	49	29.2	5.4	1,523
% of Total Calories			25	5	

* *Note:* Quantities given indicate nutritional value per serving.

Menu

32

Crudités Provençale

Trout Sausage on a Bed of Asparagus

Quick and Safe Chocolate Cake
with Frozen Vanilla Yogurt
and Fresh Raspberries

Crudités Provençale

*H*ere the main course is delicate both in taste and in substance, as is the bed of asparagus. By contrast I wanted a crisp and colorful first course. In southern France as well as in Italy, where the abundance and variety of fresh vegetables is legendary, crudités are frequently offered as a first course no matter what follows. In Provence, it is often presented on a tray of carved olive wood, or on a boat of cork, accompanied by several regional dips and sauces, such as aioli, anchoyade, or vinaigrette.

2 *red peppers*
2 *artichoke hearts*
2 *anchovy fillets*
2 *tablespoons freshly squeezed lemon juice*
1 *tablespoon Dijon-style mustard*
½ *cup extra virgin olive oil*

Fresh pepper
1 *head romaine, shredded*
1 *fennel bulb, trimmed (cutting off the stems down to the bulb) washed and cut into sticks lengthwise*
4 *ounces Greek black olives, pitted*

Char red peppers over flame until skin is blackened. (If you do not have access to a flame—from your stove, or an outdoor grill—bake peppers in an oven at 375°F until skin cracks all around.) Cut lengthwise in half. Under running cold water, peel charred skin and seeds. Pat dry. Cut skinned pepper in strips.

Cook two artichokes in boiling water for 20 minutes. Drain. Remove leaves and choke. Cut hearts into strips.

Puree anchovies with lemon juice, mustard, oil, and pepper. On serving plates, spread a bed of romaine. Place fennel, red pepper, artichoke, and black olives over romaine. Pour anchovy dressing and serve.

Trout Sausage on a Bed of Asparagus

1 pound fillet of trout
2 cakes tofu
1 tablespoon dried tarragon
4 ounces 1% cottage cheese
3 egg whites
½ teaspoon black pepper
½ cup parsley, chopped
  Sausage casings
2 tablespoons evaporated milk
¼ cup soy milk
2 tablespoons olive oil
2 shallots, minced
1 tablespoon lemon juice
¼ cup sherry wine
  Fresh pepper

In the food processor, puree fish, tofu, and tarragon. Add cottage cheese, egg whites, pepper, and parsley. Refrigerate for an hour or more.

Remove casings from their salt. Place a casing under faucet, let water run liberally for a minute to rinse out salt. Repeat with other casings. Cut casings evenly, in 4-inch lengths. Tie a knot at one end of each casing. Adjust the other open end of casing onto your sausage maker. (If you do not have an electric sausage maker, you may find manual ones in virtually every hardware store or kitchen equipment shop.)

Remove chilled trout mixture from refrigerator, feed mixture through your sausage maker, making certain to avoid air bubbles in the sausage. When casing is almost filled, remove from machine, and tie second knot to close sausage. Repeat until all fish mixture is used. With the tip of a sharp knife, prick tiny wholes on all sides of trout sausages. In a wide kettle, put 1 quart water and 2 tablespoons evaporated milk. Bring to a boil. Reduce flame to a mere simmer. Place sausages in kettle, and cook 5 minutes, until sausages rise to the surface. With a slotted spoon, remove from kettle. In a skillet, heat olive oil, and lightly brown sausages on all sides. While the asparagus steams, proceed to make the sauce.

In a saucepan, heat the olive oil, sauté the shallots until just golden, add flour and stir in soy milk. Add lemon juice and sherry wine. Season with pepper. If sauce appears too thick, add some soy milk. Turn off heat.

For the bed of asparagus

30 asparagus (approximately), peeled and trimmed
½ lemon, squeezed
2 tablespoons polyunsaturated margarine
½ cup parsley finely chopped
  Fresh pepper

In a kettle, bring 2 cups water to a boil. Place asparagus in a steamer basket and lower into kettle. Cover and cook 8 minutes or until asparagus is tender. (Time will vary according to the size and age of the asparagus.) Melt margarine and add lemon juice. Sprinkle parsley and pepper. On each plate, divide asparagus, place sausage, pour sauce over sausage, and serve.

On each plate, place 4 to 5 asparagus, add one sausage, pour a little of the sauce over the sausage and serve.

Quick and Safe Chocolate Cake with Frozen Vanilla Yogurt and Fresh Raspberries

10 ounce package semi-sweet baking chocolate

1 tablespoon decaffeinated coffee

1 cup vanilla soy milk

2 tablespoons flour

12 tablespoons polyunsaturated margarine, or soy butter

1 tablespoon sugar

4 egg whites, beaten stiff

1 pint frozen vanilla yogurt

1 pint fresh raspberries

Preheat the oven to 350°F. Line a springform pan with wax paper, set aside. In an ovenproof bowl, mix the chocolate and the coffee, and place in the oven until mixture melts. In a small saucepan, over medium flame, heat 3 tablespoons soy milk mixed with one tablespoon flour. Gradually stir in the rest of the soy milk, and cook until mixture thickens to custardlike consistency. Add melted chocolate, margarine, remaining spoonful of flour, sugar, and custard. Cook one more minute.

With a rubber spatula, gently fold in the beaten egg whites into the chocolate custard mixture. Pour cake mixture into springform. Bake for 15 minutes. Turn off the oven, leaving the cake inside, with the oven door open slightly, for another 10 minutes. Remove from oven and let cake cool 20 more minutes. This cake is best served warm but cold is good as well. Either way, served topped with the frozen yogurt and the raspberries, this elegant but simple-to-make dessert, makes for an exquisite and almost too—good-for-you conclusion to a fine meal. (*Serves 8.*)

	Calories	Cholesterol (mg)	Total Fat (g)	Saturated Fat (g)	Sodium (mg)
Crudités Provençale	329	—	33.0	4.2	419
Trout Sausage on a Bed of Asparagus	380	65	19.8	3.5	292
Quick and Safe Chocolate Cake with Frozen Vanilla Yogurt and Fresh Raspberries	438	—	32.0	7.2	34
TOTAL	1,147	65	84.8	14.9	745
% of Total Calories			67	12	

* *Note:* Quantities given indicate nutritional value per serving.

Lunches

*I*n this book I have assumed that the gourmet focus of your day will be your evening meal. But cholesterol control, as with any diet, can be achieved only if you maintain it throughout the day, at all meals. Lunches can also be tasty, healthful, and cholesterol free. Many of these lunch menus feature vegetables and fresh fruit, while those that feature fish or fowl are as light and cholesterol-safe as the vegetarian ones.

Menu

1

Steamed Vegetables with Miso Dip

Cantaloupe and Raspberries

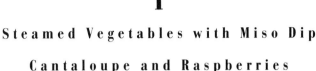

Steamed Vegetables with Miso Dip

2 Belgian endive, halved

1 large red bell pepper, trimmed, seeds removed, and quartered

1 green bell pepper, trimmed, seeds removed, and quartered

1¼ pounds green beans, trimmed

2 carrots, peeled and cut in half lengthwise

½ head broccoli, trimmed, florets separated, and stems peeled

2 celery stalks, trimmed, peeled, and cut in half lengthwise

1 red beet, cooked and sliced

2 tablespoons miso (soybean paste)

3 tablespoons water

Juice of ½ lemon

3 scallions, chopped fine

¼ teaspoon cayenne pepper

1 tablespoon light soy sauce

Prepare grill or preheat broiler (if neither is available, a frying pan with ridges on top of the stove is a fine substitute). In a kettle, bring about 2 cups of water to a boil and blanch endive for 3 minutes. Drain, then grill endive on each side for 3 minutes. Steam remaining vegetables for 5 minutes.

In a bowl, combine miso, water, lemon juice, scallions, cayenne pepper, and soy sauce. Divide miso dip among 4 small serving bowls and place each bowl in the center of a lunch plate. Place small quantities of each steamed vegetable around the bowls, making the vegetables look like flower petals. Serve.

Cantaloupe and Raspberries
◆

1 small cantaloupe, peeled and sliced
1 cup raspberries
  Few mint leaves (optional), minced

Arrange fruit on dessert plates, then sprinkle
on mint. Refrigerate and serve cool.

	Calories	Cholesterol (mg)	Total Fat (g)	Saturated Fat (g)	Sodium (mg)
Steamed Vegetables with Miso Dip	116	—	—	—	233
Cantaloupe and Raspberries	45	—	—	—	—
TOTAL	161	—	—	—	233

% of Total Calories

* *Note:* Quantities given indicate nutritional value per serving.

Cream of Parsley Soup

My Waldorf Salad

Iced Coffee Pot de Crème

Cream of Parsley Soup

2 bunches fresh parsley with stems,
   chopped
1 tablespoon olive oil
3 potatoes, diced
6 cups water
   Fresh pepper to taste
   Juice of ½ lemon

Reserve 2 tablespoons of parsley for later. In a
kettle, heat the olive oil, stir in remaining parsley, and cook over medium heat for 2 minutes.
Add the potatoes, water, and pepper. Bring to
a boil, reduce heat to low, cover, and cook for
15 minutes. Let cool a bit, then pour into
blender and puree. Return soup to kettle, and
bring back to a boil. Add lemon juice and
sprinkle with reserved parsley and serve.

My Waldorf Salad

½ cup nonfat yogurt
¼ cup 1% cottage cheese
   Juice of 1 lemon
   Fresh pepper to taste
1 teaspoon Dijon-style mustard
4 large eating apples, washed, peel
   remaining, cored and cubed
½ cup coarsely chopped walnuts or
   unsalted peanuts
½ cup peeled and diced celery
⅓ cup raisins

In a blender, combine the yogurt, cottage
cheese, lemon juice, pepper and mustard. Set
aside. In a salad bowl, mix the apples, nuts,
celery, and raisins. Add dressing, toss well,
and refrigerate.

Iced Coffee Pot de Crème

½ cup coffee

1 tablespoon coffee liqueur

2 tablespoons cornstarch

3 cups vanilla soy milk

Mix coffee, liqueur, cornstarch, and soy milk in a blender. Pour into a saucepan set over low heat and, stirring all the while, bring to a boil. Cook for a few minutes, until liquid thickens. Pour into four small individual serving dishes. Refrigerate at least 1 hour. Serve.

Note: For those of you who prefer decaffeinated coffee, feel free to use it instead of regular coffee.

	Calories	Cholesterol (mg)	Total Fat (g)	Saturated Fat (g)	Sodium (mg)
Cream of Parsley Soup	150	—	3.4	0.5	48
Waldorf Salad	232	—	8.8	—	133
Iced Coffee Pot de Crème	71	—	2.6	—	—
TOTAL	453	—	14.8	0.5	181
% of Total Calories			29	1	

* *Note:* Quantities given indicate nutritional value per serving.

Consommé Madrilène with Cucumber

Black Bean Croquettes
with Yogurt-Coriander Sauce

Honeydew Melon with Lime

Consommé Madrilène with Cucumber

*T*his consommé takes its name from the tomato that has been added to the otherwise classic clear soup; *Madrilène* simply means "from Madrid."

  2 *cucumbers, peeled and diced*
    (reserve peel)
  2 *cups water*
  6 *cups chicken consommé, homemade*
    (see Note) or canned
  2 *tablespoons tomato puree*
  1 *teaspoon dried dill*
    Fresh pepper

Note: To make your own consommé, place a 4-pound chicken, skin removed, in a soup pot. Cover with water and add 2 peeled celery stalks, 1 bay leaf, 2 peeled carrots, a few peppercorns, 1 onion stuck with 3 cloves, and pinch of salt. Bring to a boil, reduce heat, cover, and simmer for 1½ hours. Strain through a sieve. Use as needed. Freeze remaining consommé in plastic containers.

In a saucepan, cook cucumber peel with the water over low heat, covered, for 30 minutes. Discard peel. This is a *fumet*, which simply means "essence of." In a kettle, combine *fumet* with the consommé and tomato puree. Bring to a boil, reduce heat, add cucumber, dill, pepper, and cook 1 minute.

Black Bean Croquettes with Yogurt-Coriander Sauce

*

For the croquettes

2 *cups cooked or canned black beans, drained and rinsed*

1 *egg white*

1 *small onion, chopped*

1 *teaspoon Tabasco*

4 *tablespoons soft tofu*

½ *cup bread crumbs*

2 *tablespoons olive oil*

In a blender or food processor, puree beans, egg white, onion, Tabasco, and tofu. With a tablespoon, form croquettes, rolling each in bread crumbs on all sides; you should have 12 to 14 croquettes. Heat oil in a skillet over moderate heat and sauté croquettes on both sides, about 2 to 3 minutes; they should be crisp. Drain on absorbent paper.

For the sauce

8 *ounces low-fat yogurt*

8 *ounces 1% cottage cheese*

1 *cup finely chopped fresh coriander (cilantro)*

Combine ingredients for sauce. Serve in a gravy boat, along with the croquettes.

Honeydew Melon with Lime

*

1 *ripe honeydew melon*

1 *lime, cut in wedges*

Fresh mint leaves, minced

Choose a ripe melon. Both ends should be soft, and you should be able to smell the aroma. Pare the melon as you would an apple. Discard seeds. Slice, and arrange slices on a serving platter. Decorate with lime wedges. Chill. Just before serving, sprinkle mint leaves.

	Calories	Cholesterol (mg)	Total Fat (g)	Saturated Fat (g)	Sodium (mg)
Consommé Madrilène with Cucumber	112	—	4.5	—	1,368
Black Bean Croquettes with Yogurt-Coriander Sauce	317	3.5	9.8	1.3	642
Honeydew Melon with Lime	55	—	—	—	—
TOTAL	484	3.5	14.3	1.3	2,010
% of Total Calories			27	2	

* *Note:* Quantities given indicate nutritional value per serving.

Menu

4

Potage of Vegetables

Salad of Tomatoes with Basil
and Sautéed Tofu

Apricot Custard

Potage of Vegetables

3 carrots, peeled and sliced

2 potatoes, diced

2 celery stalks, peeled and diced

1 leek, trimmed and julienned

1 onion, minced

1 cup finely chopped fresh parsley

1 teaspoon dried tarragon

1 bay leaf

½ teaspoon dried thyme

3 quarts water

1 teaspoon freshly grated nutmeg

Fresh pepper to taste

In a large kettle, combine all ingredients. Bring to a boil, cover, and cook for 15 minutes. With a slotted spoon, remove about a third of the vegetables and puree in a blender. Return to kettle, mixing well the vegetable puree with the rest of the soup. Return to a boil, serve.

Salad of Tomatoes with Basil and Sautéed Tofu

4 tablespoons olive oil

8 ounces firm tofu, sliced

1 garlic clove, mashed

1 teaspoon dried oregano

Fresh pepper

3 ripe tomatoes, peeled and sliced

1 cup basil leaves, left whole

1 tablespoon balsamic vinegar

In a skillet, heat 1 tablespoon of the olive oil and sauté the tofu on both sides. Add the garlic, oregano, and pepper. Arrange tomato slices, basil leaves, and tofu in an attractive pattern on a serving platter. Pour on remaining oil and vinegar and sprinkle with more pepper.

Apricot Custard

•

1 cup dried apricots, soaked
   overnight in water to cover
6 tablespoons apricot liqueur
8 ounces tofu
1 tablespoon honey

Simmer the apricots in their water until soft.
Add liqueur, then transfer to a blender and
puree along with tofu and honey. Pour into a
serving bowl, refrigerate, then serve.

	Calories	Cholesterol (mg)	Total Fat (g)	Saturated Fat (g)	Sodium (mg)
Potage of Vegetables	105	—	—	—	9
Salad of Tomatoes with Basil and Sautéed Tofu	181	—	15.9	1.8	4
Apricot Custard	186	—	2.4	—	—
TOTAL	472	—	18.3	1.8	13
% of Total Calories			35	3	

* *Note:* Quantities given indicate nutritional value per serving.

Menu

5

Cream of Carrot Soup

Brochette of Scallops and Broccoli with Lemon

Pears with Chocolate Sauce

Cream of Carrot Soup

·

1 tablespoon olive oil
2 onions, minced
8 carrots, peeled and sliced
1 teaspoon freshly grated nutmeg
6 cups chicken consommé or water
1 cup low-fat yogurt
  Fresh pepper
½ cup finely chopped scallions

In a kettle, heat olive oil and sauté onions until translucent. Add the carrots, nutmeg, and consommé or water. Bring to a boil, reduce heat to medium, cover, and cook for 12 minutes. Let cool 20 minutes, then puree in a blender. Return to kettle. If soup is too thick, add a little water. Bring back to a boil, stir in the yogurt, pepper, and scallions, then serve.

Brochette of Scallops and Broccoli with Lemon

·

1 pound bay scallops
2 lemons, sliced
1 pound broccoli, trimmed, separated in florets, and steamed for 2 minutes
2 tablespoons olive oil
1 teaspoon ground cumin
1 teaspoon sweet paprika
1 teaspoon dried dill
  Fresh pepper
1 teaspoon grated fresh ginger
  Juice of ½ lemon

Preheat the broiler. Alternate the scallops, lemon slices, and broccoli on 4 skewers. In a saucepan, heat the olive oil and sauté the cumin, paprika, dill, pepper, and ginger for a few seconds. Add lemon juice, then pour over scallops and broccoli. Broil 2 minutes on each side.

Pears with Chocolate Sauce

4 *ounces bitter or semisweet chocolate*

2 *tablespoons vanilla soy milk*

3 *pears—your choice of variety— peeled, cored, and sliced*

⅓ *cup slivered almonds*

In a double boiler, melt chocolate with soy milk.

In a dessert bowl, toss sliced pears with melted chocolate. Sprinkle on almonds, chill, and serve.

	Calories	Cholesterol (mg)	Total Fat (g)	Saturated Fat (g)	Sodium (mg)
Cream of Carrot Soup	233	0.5	8.9	0.5	1,400
Brochette of Scallops and Broccoli with Lemon	205	37.0	7.6	1.0	205
Pears with Chocolate Sauce	259	—	15.6	16.7	2
TOTAL	697	37.5	32.1	18.2	1,607
% of Total Calories			41	11	

* *Note:* Quantities given indicate nutritional value per serving.

Menu

6

Black Bean Soup with Sherry

My Caesar Salad

Green Tea Sorbet

Black Bean Soup with Sherry

2 cups black beans, soaked in water
  to cover
1 cup finely chopped fresh parsley
1 large onion stuck with 3 whole
  cloves
1 carrot, peeled and diced
¼ teaspoon dried thyme
½ teaspoon freshly grated nutmeg
  Fresh pepper to taste
5 cups water
⅔ cup sherry
1 lemon, sliced
3 hard-boiled egg whites, chopped

Discard water from beans. Put beans in a kettle, along with half the parsley, and the onion, carrot, thyme, nutmeg, pepper, and water. Bring to a boil, reduce heat to low, cover, and cook for 1 hour.

Puree soup in a blender, then return to kettle and bring back to a boil. Add sherry. Transfer to a soup terrine, add lemon slices and egg white, as well as remaining parsley. Serve.

My Caesar Salad

1 (2-ounce) can anchovy filets
2 egg whites
  Juice of ½ lemon
1 tablespoon Dijon-style mustard
2 tablespoons low-fat yogurt
3 tablespoons olive oil
4 slices whole wheat bread, cut into
  cubes
2 garlic cloves, minced
1 large or 2 medium heads romaine
  lettuce, leaves separated
1 red bell pepper, roasted, peeled,
  and sliced
¼ cup Parmesan cheese, grated
  Fresh pepper

In a blender, puree anchovies, egg whites, lemon juice, mustard, yogurt, and 2 tablespoons olive oil. Set aside.

Roast the bread cubes in a 375°F oven for about 10 to 15 minutes, or until golden brown. Pour remaining olive oil and minced garlic over bread cubes, then toss well.

Arrange romaine leaves in a salad bowl. Pour anchovy sauce over leaves, add croutons, and sprinkle on red pepper. Sprinkle cheese and pepper over and serve.

117

Lunches Menu 6

Green Tea Sorbet

1 cup water
½ cup granulated sugar
½ cup confectioners' sugar
2 egg whites, beaten until stiff
2 cups strong green tea
Juice of 1 lemon
Few sprigs of fresh mint

Make a sugar syrup by cooking the water with the granulated sugar over low heat until thick, about 10 minutes. The syrup must remain transparent; do not let it darken. Cool.

Fold confectioners' sugar gently into the egg whites. Over a double boiler, cook egg white mixture for about 10 minutes, or until firm, smooth, and shiny.

In a bowl, mix sugar syrup, tea, and lemon juice. Place bowl in the freezer for 30 minutes. In another bowl, freeze the meringue. After 30 minutes, remove both bowls from the freezer and combine contents. Replace in freezer for at least 4 hours. Serve with mint sprigs.

Note: If you have an ice-cream maker, follow instructions for making sorbet, using the same ingredients.

	Calories	Cholesterol (mg)	Total Fat (g)	Saturated Fat (g)	Sodium (mg)
Black Bean Soup with Sherry	405	—	1.0	—	38
My Caesar Salad	294	14	15.9	3.4	1,215
Green Tea Sorbet	158	—	—	—	25
TOTAL	857	14	16.9	3.4	1,278
% of Total Calories			18	3.6	

* *Note:* Quantities given indicate nutritional value per serving.

Rolled Chicken Breasts
with Asparagus Tips in Lemon Sauce

Kiwifruit Sorbet

Rolled Chicken Breasts
with Asparagus Tips in Lemon Sauce

4 whole chicken breasts, skin off,
   pounded flat

12 asparagus tips

1 teaspoon olive oil

1 teaspoon cornstarch

½ cup unflavored soy milk
   Juice of 1 lemon

1 teaspoon dried tarragon

½ cup finely chopped fresh parsley
   Fresh pepper

In the center of each flattened chicken piece, arrange 3 asparagus tips. Roll up the breasts and wrap in waxed paper; tie with a piece of string. Bring about 2 quarts of water to a boil in a large kettle. Drop in the chicken rolls, reduce heat to medium, and cook 15 minutes. Remove.

In a saucepan, heat the olive oil and stir in the cornstarch. Gradually add soy milk, stirring all the while until it thickens. Add lemon juice, tarragon, parsley, and pepper.

Unwrap chicken rolls and place on a serving platter. Pour lemon sauce over rolls and serve.

Kiwifruit Sorbet

—•—

1 cup water
½ cup granulated sugar
2 egg whites, beaten until stiff
2 tablespoons confectioners' sugar
8 ripe kiwifruit, peeled and pureed
   Juice of 1 lemon

Make the sugar syrup by heating water and sugar in a saucepan. Bring to a boil, reduce heat, and cook until thickened. Let cool.

In a double boiler, cook egg whites with the confectioners' sugar until shiny and firm. Transfer to a bowl and freeze for 30 minutes. Add pureed kiwifruit to syrup. Add lemon juice and pour into another bowl; freeze for 30 minutes.

Remove bowls from freezer and combine. Freeze again for at least 4 hours.

	Calories	Cholesterol (mg)	Total Fat (g)	Saturated Fat (g)	Sodium (mg)
Rolled Chicken Breasts with Asparagus Tips in Lemon Sauce	205	85	6.0	1.5	80
Kiwifruit Sorbet	201	—	—	—	25
TOTAL	406	85	6.0	1.5	105
% of Total Calories			13	3	

* *Note:* Quantities given indicate nutritional value per serving.

The (Almost) No Cholesterol Gourmet Cookbook

8

**Red and Yellow Peppers
with Miniature Mozzarellas
on a Bed of Arugula**

Sliced Pineapple

Red and Yellow Peppers
with Miniature Mozzarellas
on a Bed of Arugula

•

  2 *bunches arugula, shredded*
  1 *red bell pepper, seeded and diced*
  1 *medium-size red onion, chopped*
  1 *yellow bell pepper, seeded and
     diced*
  1 *pound small mozzarella balls*
½ *cup chopped fresh basil*
  1 *teaspoon dried oregano*
1½ *tablespoons balsamic vinegar*
  3 *tablespoons olive oil*
     Fresh pepper

On a serving platter, arrange the bed of arugula. Make a ring of red pepper on the arugula,
another ring of onion, then the yellow pepper.
Place the mozzarella balls in the center. Sprinkle on the basil and oregano. Make a vinaigrette from the vinegar and oil and season with
pepper. Drizzle over platter.

Sliced Pineapple

•

  1 *ripe pineapple*

Peel and slice pineapple. Serve chilled.

	Calories	Cholesterol (mg)	Total Fat (g)	Saturated Fat (g)	Sodium (mg)
Red and Yellow Peppers with Miniature Mozzarellas on a Bed of Arugula	451	88	24.4	14.8	424
Sliced Pineapple	77	—	0.7	—	—
TOTAL	528	88	25.1	14.8	424
% of Total Calories			43	25	

* *Note:* Quantities given indicate nutritional value per serving.

Menu
9

Warm Haricots Verts with Black Truffles
in Sherry Vinaigrette

Strawberry Soup

Warm Haricots Verts with Black Truffles in Sherry Vinaigrette

1 pound haricots verts (very thin
  green beans), trimmed, and steamed
  for 5 minutes
2 canned black truffles, with their
  skins and juice, chopped fine
1 tablespoon sherry vinegar
3 tablespoons hazelnut oil
  Fresh pepper

Combine all ingredients in a salad bowl, mix
well, and serve.

Strawberry Soup

1 pound fresh strawberries, hulled
10 mint leaves
2 cups dessert white wine, such as
  Sauternes or Beaumes de Venise
  Juice of 1 lemon
3 tablespoons honey

In a glass bowl, combine all ingredients. Refrigerate at least 1 hour, then serve.

	Calories	Cholesterol (mg)	Total Fat (g)	Saturated Fat (g)	Sodium (mg)
Warm Haricots Verts with Black Truffles in Sherry Vinaigrette	115	—	10	1.4	—
Strawberry Soup	170	—	—	—	—
TOTAL	285	—	10	1.4	—
% of Total Calories			32	4	

* *Note:* Quantities given indicate nutritional value per serving.

The (Almost) No Cholesterol Gourmet Cookbook

Menu

10

Onion Tart

Fennel Salad

Three-Melon Salad with Mint

Onion Tart

- 6 *sheets filo dough*
- 1 *tablespoon olive oil, plus additional to brush dough*
- 5 *onions, chopped*
- 1 *teaspoon cornstarch*
- 1 *tablespoon soy milk*
  Fresh pepper to taste
- ½ *cup chopped fresh parsley*

Preheat the oven to 375°F. Line an 8-inch pie pan with the filo sheets, lightly oiling each sheet. Bake for 15 minutes.

In a skillet, heat the olive oil and sauté the onions until golden. Stir in the cornstarch and soy milk. Add pepper. Puree mixture in a blender or food processor. Spread crust with onion mixture, then return to oven and bake for another 15 minutes. Sprinkle tart with parsley and serve.

Fennel Salad

- 2 *fennel bulbs, trimmed and sliced in fine strips*
- 1½ *tablespoons freshly squeezed lemon juice*
- 1 *tablespoon Dijon-style mustard*
- 3 *to 4 tablespoons olive oil*
- ½ *cup fresh chopped parsley*
- ½ *teaspoon freshly ground black pepper*

In a salad bowl, toss the fennel and parsley together with the dressing. Serve.

Three-Melon Salad with Mint

◆

½ *cantaloupe, flesh scooped out in balls*

½ *honeydew melon, flesh scooped out in balls*

2 *cups watermelon balls*

Juice of ½ lime

½ *cup chopped fresh mint*

Combine in a dessert bowl the 3 melons with lime juice. Refrigerate. Sprinkle with mint and serve.

	Calories	Cholesterol (mg)	Total Fat (g)	Saturated Fat (g)	Sodium (mg)
Onion Tart	68	—	3.7	0.5	48
Fennel Salad	135	—	13.8	1.8	114
Three-Melon Salad with Mint	115	—	—	—	—
TOTAL	318	—	17.5	2.3	162
% of Total Calories			49	7	

* Note: Quantities given indicate nutritional value per serving.

A Note About Breakfasts

As someone brought up in France—where breakfast consists of café au lait, croissants, or tartines au beurre (buttered slices of French bread)—I am always amazed and impressed by the richness and variety of American breakfasts. Eggs and bacon—or eggs and sausage, or eggs and ham, not to mention eggs Benedict—are almost as sacred as apple pie. And to them the buttered toast that has to accompany these dishes, and the cream in coffee, and it's no wonder the American breakfast is dangerous. But with our new cholesterol awareness, this hallowed tradition also has to be dealt with in the context of a full day's diet.

Breakfast can be our downfall or the foundation for a healthful day. Breakfast need not be less pleasurable than before. But it does mean that we have to rethink some of the breakfast clichés that we have all been brought up on.

The focus of this book, quite rightly, is on dinner, which should be the pleasurable and relaxed meal of the day. But it is obvious that controlling cholesterol is not merely a dinnertime preoccupation. It is something that has to be thought of totally, taking three daily meals into consideration. Breakfast is a good —and obvious—place to start. Here are some recommendations for breakfast:

1. Any fruit juices and fresh fruit.

2. Bran muffins, whole wheat rolls, and wheat toast made with minimal amounts of butter or saturated fats.

3. Oatmeal, oat bran, and cream of wheat hot cereals, with skim milk.

4. Commercial dry cereals. While dry cereals can be boring, what is fun and creative—not to mention healthful—is to mix five or six of them to combine taste, crunchiness, and sweetness. Get cereals that are natural—that is, those that are mostly carbohydrates rather than refined sugars. Read labels, even those on cereals that tout themselves as "natural," to make sure they are free of saturated fats (such as found in coconut, coconut oil, palm or palm kernel oils, etc.).

5. Switch from butter to margarine. You will be surprised at how good some cholesterol-free butter substitutes can be. Choose margarine in tubs over stick margarine, since they can be lower in calories and have less saturated—harmful—fat.

6. Switch from whole milk to low-fat or skim milk.

If these suggestions seem less than seductive, let me reassure you. After more than a year of savoring our new breakfast menus, I now enjoy my early-morning repasts as much as ever, and I know that I am better and healthier for it. But for those of you who refuse to give up your morning eggs and sausage, there's help. I counted myself among your number, and so I devised substitutes that satisfy breakfast cravings and are lower in cholesterol at the same time.

Apple and Turkey Sausages

This sausage is a delicious replacement for the traditional version.

- *1 pound ground turkey breast*
- *3 egg whites mixed with 4 tablespoons evaporated skim milk*
- *1 small onion, chopped*
- *½ cup chopped fresh parsley*
- *½ teaspoon fennel seeds*
- *6 tablespoons polyunsaturated margarine*
- *2 tablespoons tofu*
- *½ teaspoon ground black pepper*
- *1 apple, cored and cubed*
- *½ cup unbleached all-purpose flour*
- *2 tablespoons olive oil*

In a food processor or blender, mix first 8 ingredients. Transfer to a bowl and mix in the apple cubes. With your hands, form small patties and roll in flour. Let sausages rest, covered with a towel or plastic wrap, in refrigerator for 30 minutes.

In a skillet, heat the oil. Over medium heat, cook the sausages on both sides until light brown. Drain on absorbent paper, then serve.

Oat Bran Muffins

In recent years, doctors and nutritionists have praised the virtues of oat bran as a means of lowering cholesterol. Obviously, there are many recipes for bran muffins, and I have tried most. Some are fine, and many taste like straw. I experimented with various ingredients until I settled on the following, which produces not only palatable but down-right delicious muffins. (Makes 24.)

- *3 cups oat bran cereal*
- *3 egg whites*
- *3 tablespoons peanut oil*
- *½ cup honey*
- *2 carrots, grated*
- *1 banana*
- *½ teaspoon anise seed*
- *2 teaspoons ground cinnamon*
- *1½ cups skim milk*
- *1 tablespoon grated fresh ginger*
- *1 tablespoon baking powder*
- *½ teaspoon salt*
- *½ cup raisins*
- *½ cup chopped walnuts*
- *2 tablespoons sugar mixed with 1 tablespoon cinnamon, for top*

Preheat the oven to 400°F. By hand or in a food processor, combine all ingredients except the raisins, walnuts, and topping. When batter is smooth, add raisins and walnuts. Grease a muffin tin or place baking paper cups in the hollows of the pan. Pour batter into cups, filling to the top. Sprinkle sugar-cinnamon over and bake for 25 minutes. Let cool briefly, then remove muffins from the tin, leaving them in the paper cups, and serve warm.

One-Eyed Scrambled Eggs

•

*E*ggs are anathema on a low-cholesterol diet. The sad fact, as we are now well aware, is that egg yolks contain an unacceptably high amount of cholesterol. Thus, fried or poached eggs are on the forbidden list. But that does not mean you have to do without eggs every morning of your life. As you saw earlier, I have devised an omelette using a single yolk for four people, which translates roughly to only 40 milligrams of cholesterol per person. (Some restaurants, I am told, have devised a yolkless omelette using only egg whites, but having experimented in that vein I came to the conclusion that no omelette is better than one without yolks.) Served with my Apple and Turkey sausage, it will remind you of "pre-cholesterol" days without dire consequences.

    6 medium-size egg whites
    1 whole egg
    3 tablespoons evaporated skim milk
    ¼ cup fresh skim milk
    1 tablespoon polyunsaturated
       margarine
    ¼ teaspoon pepper

Mix egg whites, whole egg, and milks in a bowl. In a skillet set over medium heat, melt the margarine. Pour in eggs and cook, scrambling as desired. Season with pepper and serve piping hot.

	Calories	Cholesterol (mg)	Total Fat (g)	Saturated Fat (g)	Sodium (mg)
Apple and Turkey Sausages	566	97.0	38.8	8.9	410
Oat Bran Muffins	112	0.3	4.0	0.4	80
One-Eyed Scrambled Eggs	84	69.0	4.3	1.0	153

* *Note:* Quantities given indicate nutritional value per serving.

Finger Food

*A*s I have stressed, cholesterol control is a full-time preoccupation. One of the times of the day when backsliding is most common is the cocktail hour.

I have nothing against alcohol. Social drinking, in moderation, is one of civilized life's pleasures. But cocktail snacks can be dangerous, either in and of themselves or via the sauces and dips that often accompany pre-dinner dainties.

Here, too, healthful, low-cholesterol substitutes are easily found and commonly available. I offer a number that are both tasty and safe, to help you learn how to adapt finger food to a low-cholesterol regime.

One of my favorite snacks these days is a variety of fresh vegetables, cut and ready to eat in the refrigerator, such as carrots (peeled, trimmed, but left whole), celery stalks, green and red bell peppers (cut into 1-inch pieces or strips), sliced cucumbers, broccoli florets, turnips (sliced), cherry tomatoes, and fennel (peeled and cut in chunks). Any one of my dips (pages 133, 134) is a delicious accompaniment for the vegetables.

The (Almost) No Cholesterol Gourmet Cookbook

Vegetable Balls in a Piquant Sauce

For the balls

2 carrots, peeled and cut in chunks

½ head broccoli, separated and stems peeled

1 onion

1 potato, peeled and diced

½ cup chopped fresh dill

½ cup chopped fresh parsley

2 egg whites

1½ cups bread crumbs

2 tablespoons olive oil

For the sauce

12 ounces 1 percent cottage cheese

4 scallions, chopped

½ cup chopped fresh coriander (cilantro)

1 garlic clove

½ teaspoon cayenne pepper

In a food processor or blender, puree first 7 ingredients, reserving 1 cup bread crumbs. Refrigerate for 30 minutes. With your hands, form little balls the size of large marbles. Roll balls in remaining crumbs. In a skillet, heat the olive oil over medium heat and cook vegetable balls until crisp on all sides. Drain on absorbent paper.

To prepare the sauce, puree all ingredients in a food processor or blender. Pour into a serving bowl.

Insert toothpicks in vegetable balls and serve with sauce.

Tapenade

This rich but safe Provençal dish is a marvelous pâté substitute. Serve it with brown rice or oat-bran crackers and celery stalks cut in 1-inch pieces.

24 black olives, brine cured, pitted

8 anchovy filets

2 tablespoons capers

Juice of ½ lemon

2 tablespoons olive oil

1 cup tuna fish packed in water, drained

In a food processor, puree all ingredients. Transfer to a serving bowl and refrigerate. Serve with low-cholesterol crackers.

Curried Seafood on Mushrooms and Cucumber Slices

2 celery stalks, peeled and chopped fine

½ pound sealegs, chopped

1 cup low-fat yogurt

2 tablespoons Dijon-style mustard

1 tablespoon olive oil

1 tablespoon curry powder

½ cup chopped fresh dill

½ pound button mushrooms, caps only

1 cucumber, peeled and sliced

Parsley, for garnish

Paprika, for garnish

In a bowl, mix the celery, sealegs, yogurt, mustard, oil, curry powder, and dill until well mixed. Spoon a little of the salad onto mushroom caps and spread on cucumber slices. Chill. Sprinkle some parsley or paprika for decoration.

Chick Pea Dip

1 pound chick peas, soaked in water
    to cover and drained
    Juice of 1 lemon
½ cup olive oil, approximately
3 garlic cloves
½ teaspoon coriander seeds
½ cup chopped fresh coriander
    (cilantro)
2 tablespoons sesame paste
    (optional)
¼ teaspoon cayenne pepper
2 tablespoons pine nuts (optional)
4 pita breads, cut in 1-inch wedges
    and warmed

In a kettle, bring about 2 quarts of water to a
boil. Reduce heat and cook chick peas, covered, until tender for 1½ to 2 hours (you may
have to add water). Drain.

In a food processor or blender, puree chick
peas with lemon juice, oil, garlic, coriander
seeds, most of the coriander (reserve some for
decoration), sesame paste, and cayenne pepper. Transfer to a serving bowl, garnish with
pine nuts, and serve with warm pita bread.

Eggplant Caviar

1 eggplant
    Juice of 1 lemon
1 onion, peeled and chopped
1 cup chopped fresh parsley

Over a flame, char the eggplant all over until
skin cracks. (Don't be deterred if, at this point,
the eggplant looks miserable.) Under cold running water, peel off skin. Pat dry with paper
towel. Or, if you prefer a less smokey flavor,
bake eggplant in a 375°F, oven until soft. In a
food processor or blender, puree eggplant with

remaining ingredients. Transfer to a serving
bowl. Serve with pita bread or oat-bran crackers.

My Taramosalata

3 ounces taramosalata (carp row,
    obtainable in specialty stores)
4 tablespoons firm tofu
    Juice of 1 lemon
1 small onion, chopped
½ cup olive oil, approximately

In a food processor, puree all ingredients.
Taste and correct seasoning; it may require
more lemon juice or more olive oil. Transfer to
a serving bowl and serve with pita or low-
cholesterol crackers.

Swedish Meatballs

For the meatballs

1 pound ground turkey breast
2 egg whites
2 tablespoons evaporated skim milk
1 cup chopped fresh parsley
1 onion, chopped
2 garlic cloves, peeled
    Fresh pepper
1 cup bread crumbs
2 tablespoons olive oil or
    polyunsaturated margarine

For the sauce

1 tablespoon olive oil
1 small onion
1 cup soy milk in which 2 teaspoons
    cornstarch have been dissolved
½ cup chopped fresh parsley
½ teaspoon sweet paprika
1 tablespoon brandy

The (Almost) No Cholesterol Gourmet Cookbook

In a mixing bowl, combine first 8 ingredients, reserving ½ cup bread crumbs. Form little balls the size of large marbles and roll in the remaining crumbs. In a skillet, heat the oil, reduce heat, and cook meatballs for 20 minutes, turning so they brown on all sides.

In a small saucepan, heat the oil for the sauce and sauté onion until light brown. Stir in the soy milk mixture and cook for 2 minutes, stirring well. Add parsley, paprika, and brandy. Liquify in a blender and pour sauce over meatballs. Mix well and serve, inserting a toothpick in each meatball.

Miniature Bruschetta
(Roman Garlic Bread)

4 *slices whole wheat bread*
1 *garlic clove*
1 *tomato, peeled and diced*
   Ground pepper

Toast the bread, rub garlic on toast, and drizzle a little olive oil over slices. Spread with tomato and sprinkle on pepper. Cut toast into ½-inch pieces, insert toothpicks, and serve.

	Calories	Cholesterol (mg)	Total Fat (g)	Saturated Fat (g)	Sodium (mg)
Vegetable Balls in a Piquant Sauce	351	4.0	9.4	1.9	684
Tapenade	191	—	10.8	1.4	1,076
Curried Seafood on Mushrooms and Cucumber Slices	163	15.0	5.2	1.0	762
Chick Pea Dip	606	—	37	4.8	231
Eggplant Caviar	45	—	0.2	—	8
My Taramosalata	328	124.0	32.0	3.8	317
Swedish Meatballs	390	47.0	14.3	2.3	355
Miniature Bruschetta	77	—	1.0	—	143

Index